WINNING WAYS

The Funeral Profession's
Guide to Human Relations

Appleton & Lange
Stamford, Connecticut

Copyright © 1999 by Appleton & Lange
A Simon & Schuster Company

www.appletonlange.com

99 00 01 02 03 / 10 9 8 7 6 5 4 3 2 1

Prentice Hall International (UK) Limited, *London*
Prentice Hall of Australia Pty. Limited, *Sydney*
Prentice Hall Canada, Inc., *Toronto*
Prentice Hall Hispanoamericana, S.A., *Mexico*
Prentice Hall of India Private Limited, *New Delhi*
Prentice Hall of Japan, Inc., *Tokyo*
Simon & Schuster Asia Pte. Ltd., *Singapore*
Editora Prentice Hall do Brasil Ltda., *Rio de Janeiro*
Prentice Hall, *Upper Saddle River, New Jersey*

Library of Congress Cataloging-in-Publication Data
Van Beck, Todd W.
    Winning ways : the funeral profession's guide to human relations /
Todd W. Van Beck.
        p.   cm.
    ISBN 0-8385-9646-0 (pbk. : alk. paper)
        1. Undertakers and undertaking—Pratice.   2. Mourning etiquette.
    3. Interpersonal communication.   4. Interpersonal relations.
    5. Funeral rites and ceremonies.   I. Title.
    RA622.V36   1998
    363.7′5—dc21   98-3197

Acquisitions Editor: Kimberly Davies
Production Editor: Lisa M. Guidone
Production Service: Rainbow Graphics
Designer: Libby Schmitz

0-8385-9646-0

9 780838 596463

90000

PRINTED IN THE UNITED STATES OF AMERICA

This book is dedicated to Mayree L. Van Beck
1891–1976

It is also dedicated to the thousands of funeral directors here and abroad with whom it has been my good fortune to have been associated over the years. In particular, I want to recognize the following mentors, who had a profound influence on me early in my career: Norbert L. Blust, Cornelius P. Heafey, John C. Heafey, Thomas P. Heafey, A. Mervin Breland, Burdette K. Roland, Alfred B. Marsh, John B. Turner, and the Rev. Dr. Edgar N. Jackson.

CONTENTS

SECTION III. DIFFICULT SITUATIONS

SECTION IV. FUNERAL DIRECTOR SKILLS

SECTION V. COMMUNICATING WITH FAMILIES

SECTION VI.   FUNERAL SERVICE ETIQUETTE

SECTION VII.   OUR NOBLE PROFESSION
(INSPIRATIONAL READINGS ABOUT FUNERAL SERVICE)

FOREWORD

Most of us have seen the many faces of death. We have witnessed the natural death of the old and the tragic death of the young with its heartbreaking variations. These are the difficult and trying experiences of our respective professions. We are expected to offer counseling, comfort, and consolation when we ourselves are stricken by the loss or feel inept in dealing tactfully and successfully with those in torturous despair.

I have often pondered the mystery of death while sitting at the bedside of a member of my family, a friend, or a patient, watching the slow retreat from life until that final, awful moment of transition when the heart stops beating, lungs no longer breathe, eyes no longer see, lips no longer smile, and hands have lost their power to hold and to squeeze.

It is a moment of bereavement and bewilderment. Yet, it is the chosen career of mortuary science students, practicing funeral directors, and cemeterians. How, then, in Todd W. Van Beck's words, do we "promote a closer relationship between ourselves and clients who seek our assistance when death enters their lives?"

No one is more ably equipped to inspire and guide in more effective relationships than Todd. With over three decades of devoted experience as a funeral director and teacher, his remarkable human qualities have made him a mentor and guide to legions in the death care profession. His clear mind and judicious perspective have made him perhaps the most sought-after speaker in the field. Wherever he has sowed his talents, his listeners have reaped the rewards of his vast knowledge and unrivaled power of communication. One cannot help but be drawn to his marvelous intelligence and wit. He has a capacity for making connections across lines of psychology, history, and philosophy, like no one else I know. To read and hear him is like witnessing a trapeze artist who lets go of one rope and gracefully takes hold of another without a slip.

We first met when I lectured to his class in mortuary science school. His moral and intellectual quality were immediately evidenced. From his prior theological training, he brought a fierce integrity, strong convictions, and an unswerving commitment to right as he saw the right. Funeral service for him was not a job but a ministry for the mysteries of life. Over the years, Todd has become my close friend and colleague. I can only recall the sacred text, *The Ethics of the Fathers:* "Much have I learned from my teachers but more I have learned from my students." Thirty years later, Todd has become my teacher, my *rabbi*.

As a clergyperson, grief therapist, and author of several dozen volumes concerning crisis intervention, I am keenly interested in materials that assist professionals who help those who "walk through the valley of the shadow of death." Never have I been more impressed than with *Winning Ways: The Funeral Profession's Guide to Human Relations*.

Todd writes powerfully, with discerning understanding coupled with compelling practical advice. His gift of insight is profound. Yet, the style is neither complex nor esoteric. He helps us to discover new meanings through dramatic stories and piercing images. It is a triumphant volume, a harvest of redemptive thought that is destined to become a classic in the penetrating understanding of our human existence.

Rabbi Earl A. Grollman, DHL, DD
February 15, 1998

PREFACE

This work is the result of 30 years of experience in the funeral service profession. During those years, I have had the privilege to work with people from funeral homes, both large and small; colleges of mortuary science; thousands of funeral directors; cemeteries; clergy; advanced planners; aftercare coordinators; and other allied professionals across the United States and abroad.

The principle of this book is simple—helping people address the challenge of getting along with others and winning their goodwill and cooperation in everyday business and social contacts. No matter who we are or what we do, it is of particular advantage to us to be able to establish and maintain healthy, meaningful relationships.

When I began writing this book, I wanted to capture the practical, commonsense aspects of relationship-building and maintenance. The result is a book that is multidimensional and practical. It can easily be adapted for use in mortuary science training courses, staff improvement training, seminars and workshops, or for our own personal self-improvement.

Each chapter begins with learning objectives and ends with discussion questions, and each chapter promotes a theory or idea and contains a story or anecdote to further reinforce the concept.

Every human being desires respect, support, and admiration from others. It seems that being liked is a deep-seated need in most of human psychology. We want others to think well of our thoughts, ideas, and behavior. I have discovered that nothing in life is as interesting to people as other people.

This book was designed to help you meet the challenges of relating to other people. This ability will be a particularly important portion of your success formula. Your continual success and the success of your personal and professional life depend largely on your healthy and meaningful relationships. I hope you find this information helps you achieve that goal.

Todd W. Van Beck
Funeral Director
Cincinnati, Ohio
January 1998

TEN WAYS THIS BOOK
WILL BENEFIT YOU

It will:

1. Give you a new mental outlook concerning your profession, inspire you with new ambitions, and help you avoid a professional rut.

2. Help you do the things that will put you at ease among all types of people, making it easier for you to win friends.

3. Help you deal tactfully and successfully with families who complain or who want to argue.

4. Help you develop the greatest of all assets in funeral service—a winning personality.

5. Show you the principles of better leadership.

6. Increase your personal influence and popularity.

7. Help you master the art of getting others to agree with your viewpoint.

8. Enable you to avoid clashing with others and make your workday more pleasant.

9. Give you a better understanding of human nature.

10. Give you greater enthusiasm for your daily work in funeral service.

I

SERVICE
EXCELLENCE

"Those who attain to any excellence commonly spend life in some one single pursuit, for excellence is not often gained upon easier terms."

samuel Johnson

THIS THING CALLED SERVICE

"There is but one virtue—the eternal sacrifice of self."

George Sand

LEARNING OBJECTIVES

- To be able to define the word *service*.

- Procedures in interpreting service needs.

- Describe your own service examples.

- Focus on how to close service gaps that exist.

GETTING DEPENDS UPON GIVING

In our efforts to win friends and clients, all of us, at times, often overlook the simplest factor in achieving these ends—doing things for others! Serving to the best of our ability! That is the all-important ingredient in the recipe for getting ahead.

Service—how often do you hear that word, particularly in the funeral service profession? The meaning of the word service today is in a type of crisis. In a society that moves as fast as we do, and is as technologically oriented as we are, the objective of serving people often gets lost in the shuffle of deadlines, Social Security numbers, and files. As many customers will testify, the spirit of the word is often lacking in the efforts of the people who are supposed to exemplify it. Many want friends and success but are more concerned about *getting* than with the idea of *giving*.

CHRISTMAS CALLS

Years ago, I worked for a veteran funeral director who was very service-minded. In fact, his concern with giving inspired him to do some creative things. When this funeral director made arrangements, he would note in a small book people that he believed would be all alone on Christmas. Then, on Christmas morning, he would call them on the phone and wish them a *Merry Christmas* and visit with them for a few minutes. He made maybe five to ten calls each year, and in time his reputation for giving was well established in the community. He did this for 50 Christmases.

The calls that this funeral director made on Christmas had a domino effect. When he made five calls, five individuals told five other people; these people told others, and eventually everyone in the community knew this funeral director as a giving person.

Every funeral home can boost its client base when everyone in it is as eager to serve as this funeral director was. Clients seek out the individual who puts him- or herself out to render satisfying service, whether it be pre-need, at-need, or post-funeral care.

"INTERPRETING" CLIENTS' NEEDS

Recently, I went to purchase a piano. I was in a shopping mall and it was about 9:00 P.M. I entered the piano gallery and the man sitting behind the desk looked at me and said, "We're closing in three minutes." Three minutes to buy a piano! I was leaving the store when a young lady came out from the back and walked up to me and said, "How can I help you?" I, in return, asked, "Aren't you closing?" She replied, "Oh, no, I'll stay to answer any questions you might have." One hour later, I purchased the piano, and I am confident that the young lady received a favorable commission.

Such wholehearted service is what binds clients to an organization and increases the prestige of the individual who gives it.

THE SPIRIT THAT WINS FRIENDS AND CUSTOMERS

Not long ago, I was told of a man who went to another city to attend a funeral. The day turned warm, so he didn't miss his topcoat which he had left hanging in the coat room of the funeral home. He returned home, not remembering where he had left his coat, and finally gave it up as lost.

Meanwhile, the apprentice at the funeral home discovered the coat. It had no identification except a blank deposit slip bearing the name of a bank and the account number. The apprentice called the bank. A bank clerk took the account number, identified the man, and called him about the coat.

The owner got his topcoat, thanks to the funeral home apprentice and the bank clerk, both of whom had a sincere desire to serve clients well!

BY SERVING OTHERS, WE SERVE OURSELVES

Undoubtedly, there are many ideas you can implement to provide better service of your funeral home. Think about them, and meet to discuss them. The possibilities will surprise you, and you can bet the firm down the street probably isn't brainstorming.

Inscribed on a sundial at Oxford University are the Latin words *periunt et impurtanture,* meaning "The hours perish and are laid to your charge." For your own best interest, as well as for the funeral home, employ your hours at work, and even some of your leisure time, thinking of better ways to give your clients higher-quality service.

 ## DISCUSSION QUESTIONS

1. What is the level of service being offered?

2. How have our service offerings changed?

3. What kind of service was offered years ago? Can we re-establish services that we abandoned?

4. What service goals can we set for today?

2

SERVICE

"Amid life's quests there seems but worthy one, to do men good."
Gamaliel Bailey

 LEARNING OBJECTIVES

- Give an example of unexpected service.
- Identify how little courtesies are important to people.
- Give examples of little courtesies.
- Explain why service and consistency are so essential.

UNEXPECTED SERVICE CAPTIVATES CLIENTS

Mackenzie King, the former Canadian Prime Minister, patronized one hatter exclusively for over 40 years. When asked why he had confined his trade, he told this story:

"When I was a young man and beginning in Canadian politics, I stepped into this little man's shop one rainy morning. My hat was much the worse for wear and so was my topcoat—in fact, I must have presented a rather seedy picture. My umbrella had a number of bends in it—rather a beggar of an umbrella which I tried to hide in a corner. I soon purchased a new hat and, noticing that the rain had ceased, reached for my umbrella. Imagine my surprise to find my umbrella rolled as neatly and as tightly as though it were the finest umbrella in all of Ottawa—all the bends skillfully hidden. That little hatter has been selling me hats for years, and upon occasion, rolls my umbrella. There is character in a man who gracefully disguises the misfortunes of his fellow man, and unasked, renders the little, unexpected services."

Rolling and unbending the umbrella for King cost the hatter nothing. In the 1890s, a true gentleman or lady paid great heed to a correctly rolled umbrella, and thus the service rendered King's shabby umbrella impressed the future Prime Minister tremendously.

The point of King's story is this: These little attentions that *cost us nothing* are really priceless in that they demonstrate more loudly than words our own character and the character of the organization we represent.

LITTLE COURTESIES ARE JUST GOOD SENSE

A funeral director who built a successful practice used this method of courtesy with every client:

When the arrangements for the funeral had been made, he would take out a small piece of stationery and in his own handwriting, along with the Statement of Goods and Services selected, would jot down the various decisions that the family had made concerning the funeral, that is, times, places, responsibilities, and the like.

He would fold the paper and, with genuine concern, hand it to a family member, saying, "This will help you remember the details of the service. I did this just for you."

Attention to minute details of courtesy and service, over and above that which the client of a funeral home expects, indicates a mental attitude on our part that the client appreciates instantly.

Never did a client look at the funeral director's note and say, "That's stupid," or "What a waste." No, never! Usually, they looked at him with thanks and admiration for his act of kindness and service.

This type of courtesy helps smooth the way in client relationships, for it helps change a negative mental attitude toward the funeral home to a positive one. The positive attitude helps clients warm up to the director because they feel that he or she is honestly interested in their well-being.

COURTESY TODAY IS UNEXPECTED

Surveys today indicate that most Americans and Canadians do not expect courtesy from clerks, business people, and the like. They *want* courtesy, but they no longer really expect it.

We can all relate to impersonal people, even rude people in the business world. When people receive courtesy, they are surprised, and when they are surprised in a positive fashion, they will remember you.

Take the example of an exclusive funeral home in New York City:

The funeral home is world famous for its first-class handling of the funerals of the rich and famous. Within this grand operation is a coat-check girl who is famous in her own way for rendering unexpected service. This is what she does: If a client's coat collar is turned up a bit, as he removes his outer wrap, she smilingly says, "Won't you please step a bit closer, sir, your coat collar's turned up," and she swiftly adjusts it.

If a button is off any overcoat checked with her, she matches it from a stock on hand, sews it on securely and places a little slip-over card on it. She writes on the card, "With Jane's compliments—and I do hope this one doesn't come off." She never mentions the service verbally, and the name of the funeral home is printed on the bottom of the card!

Many of Jane's other little services go unnoticed, but she honestly wants to be useful and lets the rewards take care of themselves.

She has been the coat-check girl for over 40 years, and today, many families continue to call this outstanding funeral home, in part because of the acts of courtesy from the coat-check girl.

This brings up a very important element in doing the little things. If they do not spring from a sincere desire to be above the ordinary in the profession, and if they come from someone who thinks of nothing but the return he or she gets *right now,* such courtesies and services will not be as effective.

HUMAN NATURE RESPONDS TO GENEROUS SERVICE

The story is told about Mark Twain staying overnight at a Boston hotel. The night was rainy; he had forgotten his overshoes, and his shoes were soaked. Guests at the hotel customarily placed their shoes outside their room door at night, to be picked up by the hall porter for shining. The next morning when the great author reached for his shoes, he was delighted to find that his shoes were perfectly dry and shined to perfection.

He immediately rang for the hall porter. Upon his arrival, Twain slid a five-dollar bill into the hand of the astonished employee. He said, "What's this for, Mr. Twain?" "You know what that's for," Twain replied. "Any man smart enough to dry my shoes after a wet night without the shoes stiffening is smart enough to know there are people in the world smart enough to show some appreciation."

The true ring of sincerity must be behind the unexpected service.

SERVICE AND CONSISTENCY: A WINNING COMBINATION

The tremendous success of a certain funeral director in the Northeast is founded entirely upon the expert rendering of the unexpected service by his workers and himself. He is committed to service day after day, month after month, year after year. If there are any of the little things in making clients comfortable that he has overlooked, he will, to this day, pay you to tell him what they are.

We, as funeral professionals, develop a finer character as we practice the fine art of thoughtfulness in every contact with the people outside our organization and those within it. The world is filled with lonely, mistreated souls who are unaccustomed to considerate service. When they receive it in your funeral home, you instantly win their goodwill. You then are a special sort of human being to them. *You* are exceptional— finer and more capable than the other funeral home down the street.

Winston Churchill once told his private secretary: "When a man renders me a service I have not asked for, *He is greater than I,* for I am in his debt and he remains the greater until I can repay."

Far from losing, when we pay attention constantly to the little courtesies we can render, we in fact win and dignify ourselves in the process. We become members of that royal line of funeral professionals who bestow favors rather than seek them.

 DISCUSSION QUESTIONS

1. Think of an example when you gave a "little, unexpected attention or courtesy" to a family.

2. How can we become more consistent with quality service?

3. Does your funeral home already do something special in the way of small courtesies that the members of your community remember?

4. If not, brainstorm about what you could start doing that would not cost anything but that would simply add a nice touch to your service.

3

WHAT DO MISTAKES COST?

"Any man may make a mistake, but none but a fool will continue in it."

Cicero

LEARNING OBJECTIVES

- Explain the dangers of mistakes in funeral service.
- Identify ways that mistakes hurt reputation.
- Identify areas in funeral services where mistakes thrive.
- Compare and contrast good news versus bad news information.

IN OUR PROFESSION, THEY ARE BETTER NEVER MADE

Among certain businesses and professions, there is a disposition to joke about making mistakes. Some people seem to think it's okay to just "laugh them off." In our profession, that attitude has no room.

Some find it convenient to quote the words of a famous American: "The man who never makes mistakes never does anything." The author of that phrase certainly did not mean to imply that he excused mistakes. He meant that the most conscientious struggler for success was bound to make mistakes, but that the accomplishments would far outweigh the natural, human errors.

"LITTLE" MISTAKES CAN BE CATASTROPHIC

People who mess up a lot are not popular—it is as simple as that. Consistent mess-ups always make work for others, and that results in resentments. Others always lose a little respect for us when we consistently make mistakes. It is worth everything to be dependable!

A large funeral was being conducted for the Archbishop of Chicago. It was a huge ceremony—statesmen, Vatican representatives; the cathedral was literally full of the rich and famous.

The Archbishop was resting in a cast-iron bronze casket that weighed over 1,400 pounds. As the Mass was being said, a funeral director was positioned outside with the church truck to place under the casket as soon as the pallbearers (there were 12 of them) had carried the heavy casket down the long stairs. The casket would then be wheeled to the awaiting funeral coach.

Television cameras, news photographers, and media commentators were everywhere. The eyes of the world were focused on that scene.

The mass ended, and the casket was being carried down the long stairs, but NO church truck. The funeral assistant had left his position and was nowhere to be found.

The pallbearers hesitated, looked around, and the procession stopped. Then, it jerked ahead to the awaiting coach. The pallbearers were exhausted and almost didn't make it. The assembly was noticeably disturbed; the funeral director was pale—and every bit of this was caught for posterity on film.

Later, the funeral assistant's excuse was that he needed a drink of water! That is a practical demonstration of the seriousness of mistakes. Even one can weaken the whole funeral structure.

MISTAKES HURT REPUTATION

This funeral assistant's thirst severely hurt the reputation of an outstanding funeral establishment. It is up to us to be sure, to be careful, to be thorough, and to be reliable!

WHERE MISTAKES THRIVE

Misquoting prices or services, giving out obsolete or misinformation, misinterpreting and giving the family something else, underpricing or overpricing, supplying a wrong-sized vault, making promises that you are not sure the goods and services can fulfill, and adding up the funeral bill wrong—these are only a few of the irritating mistakes that cause so much trouble, and cost so much money.

Why are they made? Carelessness and thoughtlessness are the principal causes, not merely the carelessness of the act itself but of "mind habits" also. The chronic mistake maker either does not have the ability to concentrate on the work or "can't be bothered" doing so.

Yet, funeral work demands and requires that contact with the public is a full-time mental job, as well as a physical one. Families are exacting and never excuse listlessness, indifference, or slipshod efforts that suggest the individual's heart is not in his or her work. Incidentally, that attitude is a fertile breeding ground for mistakes.

ATTITUDE TOWARD FAMILIES

Some of the gravest mistakes in funeral home human relations are to be found in attitude toward families in the "Oh well, what on earth do you want and let's get it over with in a hurry" attitude. In fact, this might be called the "cardinal offense," because over time it drives families away faster than perhaps any other reason.

A man in Salt Lake City wanted to talk to a funeral director about his mother's impending death. He went in early and the receptionist sat him in a sitting room. The man sat, and sat, and sat for 45 minutes. As the man rose to leave, the receptionist said, "Oh, I think the director is about ready to see you now." The enraged man looked at the receptionist and said, "Well, I am not ready or willing to see him."

For every good experience, word of mouth will tell three people; for every bad experience, word of mouth will tell 15 people! The lesson is this: Bad news travels faster and better than good news. When something bad happens, you have to work five times harder to get the good message out to the people who have heard the bad!

IT IS A MISTAKE TO PATRONIZE FAMILIES

Another great mistake is to upstage a family, that is, to be condescending toward them. You may be the seventh son of a seventh son and your ancestors may have come over on the Mayflower, and your great-great grandfather may have had the first embalmer's license, but in our profession, the only safe, secure route is to come down off any ivory towers and be a human being in your dealings with families.

The instinct of self-preservation often prompts people to deny responsibility for their errors. This never really works, for it merely adds to the original problem. We just can't alibi our blunders and get by very long. Sooner or later they catch up with us. Persistent guarding against making mistakes is high proof of loyalty to our funeral home and to our own true selves. Study each one and profit by it to the extent that at least you will not make that *one* again.

The great wise and practical American, Benjamin Franklin, once wrote, "When you profit by a mistake, you have gained a little out of an otherwise total loss!"

 DISCUSSION QUESTIONS

1. List some of the potential areas for mistake making in your funeral home. Talk about the consequences of these mistakes.

2. Since we are all human, and we do and will make mistakes, how can we avoid them?

3. How can we stay focused on positive accomplishments?

4. What kind of word of mouth does your funeral home generate?

4

YOUR ACTIONS REFLECT YOUR THOUGHTS

"Greatness in attitude is so often a courteous synonym for great success."
Philip Guedalla

LEARNING OBJECTIVES

- Give a definition for *greatness in attitude*.
- Identify and explain the power of a positive thought.
- Explain what a disciplined positive attitude means.
- Explain the danger of hypocrisy in funeral service.

OTHERS SENSE YOUR SPIRIT

A funeral home consultant had finished his study of why a particular firm was losing families. "I have discovered," he said, "why families are not calling you for your services. As hard as this fact is, it is a fact nonetheless. You no longer hold the right thought toward your families. Your cynicism and lack of warmth is evident in your funerals, and the public has sensed the change."

Families feel the thought we hold toward them. They instinctively know whether you are thinking kindly of them. They "get it" almost instantly. If your thought is cold, the family is chilled. They tighten their attitudes and probably will not be receptive to the idea of calling your firm again.

FAMILIES REFLECT YOUR ATTITUDE

A fatal situation had arisen at a funeral home. Two young funeral directors were making bets as to who could make funeral arrangements in the shortest amount of time.

A family sat in the arrangement office as one of the funeral directors raced to beat his young friend's record of 25 minutes. He was going through the arrangements in record time, if only he could finish it up before the clock hit 25 minutes. As he raced through the vital statistics, he saw that it had only taken six minutes—WOW, he was on his way.

Suddenly, the widow spoke up. "I get it," she said, "you're not interested in our problems at all, are you? All right, here's one person who will never trouble you again."

The young funeral director was stunned. He tried to make amends, but it was too late. He made a fatal error that day out of immaturity and unprofessionalism and ultimately learned the hard consequences of such an act: The family who "catches on" to a poor attitude or poor spirit of service will walk out!

GOODWILL BLOSSOMS FROM KINDLY THOUGHTS

In reading of such stupidity, most of us in funeral service are inclined to think, "How ridiculous! I certainly know more about handling families than to act that way." True enough. Nevertheless, as true professionals, we must keep a constant guard on our thought toward families.

THE MIGHTY INFLUENCE OF A POSITIVE THOUGHT

Arriving at a tour of a funeral home, one lady became terribly uncomfortable. She sat nervously in the car, looking back and forth as if she thought a ghost would pop out anytime.

Eventually, the funeral director went out to the car, smiled warmly, and cordially invited the woman to sit on the front porch of the funeral home. Eventually, through the power of his positive attitude, the lady joined the tour. She later said that she had been very squeamish about going to a funeral home, but the positive attitude of the funeral director calmed her down. You get the point. The funeral director believed in the value of the funeral and what he did for people, and this positive attitude came through like a shining light.

Funeral directors are outstanding examples of holding the right thought. They are not thinking of shortcuts. Funeral directors take the responsibility as a positive role model in death care very seriously and hence exemplify a positive attitude.

As a funeral service professional, you may find many whose appearance or actions you may not approve of, people who seem eccentric, stupid, or overly critical. Yet, to be skilled in dealing with others, you must never be prejudiced toward any real or fancied faults in them. After all, this should not be difficult; your contact with families is relatively short. You don't have to live with them. There is probably a great deal more to be admired about them than we give them credit for at first glance.

FAMILIES DESERVE THE RIGHT THOUGHT

As funeral professionals, we owe it to our families to project a disciplined positive attitude. We can all make ourselves most unhappy by fretting over annoying peculiarities in the families we serve. By minimizing annoyances and dealing with all in a spirit of excellence, patience, and charitability, we will not only enjoy our profession but will reflect an attitude that will immediately attract the goodwill of others.

If we all hold the right attitude toward our families, there will be no letdown even after the funeral is over. A recent incident demonstrates the importance of this.

A funeral home in Buffalo completed a funeral, and two funeral directors returned back to the funeral home with the funeral coach. Without their knowledge, a family member was in the flower room picking up a plant. This man was dressed unusually for the summer season. He had on a stocking cap, ear muffs, gloves, snow boots, and a winter coat, and the temperature was 95 degrees!

As the two staff funeral directors were walking back to the funeral home, they were openly and loudly discussing how weird that man looked dressed in winter clothes. The poor man heard every word.

HYPOCRISY ENDANGERS RELATIONSHIPS

The man was hurt and shocked by the actions and attitudes of the two funeral directors, for they had both been "all sweetness" at the funeral. The man was shocked by the suddenness with which the funeral director's seeming sincerity and cordiality had turned to cruel ridicule. He sought out the general manager of the funeral home and told her the story.

Realizing the seriousness of the offense, she said, "I cannot tell you how humiliated I am to hear this. It is the duty of all of us to treat everyone with the greatest respect, and to show in every way that we welcome and appreciate their trust and patronage. I shall talk to those men and correct this situation. They will learn quickly that their positions are in jeopardy. In the meantime, I shall insist that they apologize in writing."

The demonstration by the general manager of holding the right attitude immediately calmed the man and he told her to do nothing about it. Then, the man followed her lead by saying, "You are more than generous in your attitude. I feel it will be a good lesson for those men of yours!"

THE WRONG THOUGHT DEFEATS ITSELF

The great American jurist, Benjamin Cardozo, of the United States Supreme Court, once said, "It is strange how many lawyers come before me who have it in their minds that they can outsmart the Supreme Court. This thought is so evident by their actions and their pleas that all of us seem to sense it at once. We merely exchange smiles and let the wrong-thought holder defeat himself."

It is distinctly to the benefit and value of our great profession that we who make up its ranks display a positive, helpful attitude. We should strive to make it a matter of habit.

 DISCUSSION QUESTIONS

1. How do you think a professional attitude is maintained?

2. Give examples of people you know who have a positive attitude.

3. Have you ever encountered a negative attitude?

4. How do you react to a hypocrite?

5

DEPENDABILITY

*"Independence? That's middle class blasphemy. We are all
dependent on one another, every soul of us on earth."*

Pygmalion, Act V

George Bernard Shaw

 LEARNING OBJECTIVES

- Emphasize the importance of dependability in funeral service.

- Focus on the vital aspect of fulfilling instructions.

- Identify the dangers of leaning on other people.

- Explain how accurate funeral information is so important.

INDISPENSABLE IN THE FUNERAL SERVICE PROFESSION

One may have a fine personality, but in funeral service, dependability is of first importance. A dependable funeral professional arouses respect in others. The members of one's family, friends, and business associates all respond to a demonstration of that quality. Families we serve may never request it in so many words, but it is the funeral professional's dependable service that wins their respect, repeat business, and loyalty.

The world of service professionals pays its biggest rewards to dependable people, individuals with good judgment and resourcefulness enough to meet situations without unduly leaning on someone.

HE DELIVERED

The story is told of a Midwestern funeral director who, in the course of making funeral arrangements, learned that the family had a son who had been missing for over 50 years. The father had died and the mother wanted desperately to get word to her lost son.

The funeral director expressed the desire to help but made no promises that he could not keep. He made a gallant effort to contact the son, even engaging the services of a private detective. After two days of searching, the detective located the man. Unbelievably, he lived only 40 miles away.

This funeral director demonstrated superb dependability. In fact, given the number of years that most funeral homes have been in operation, it is no surprise that our profession is noted far and wide for its dependability. Today, as always, you will be no less heroic and worthy in the minds of your families when you demonstrate dependability even under trying circumstances.

FUNERAL INFORMATION MUST BE ACCURATE

Dependable funeral service to a client/family requires you to have a full knowledge and understanding of your job. The time you spend in studying the true meaning of the funeral will be time well spent. Whatever information you give, or whatever service you perform, let it be accurate. Nothing more quickly cools a family from dealing further with us than when we provide inaccurate information or services that turn out to be faulty, or when we are ineffective and produce mistakes that are annoying or costly to the family.

We all make mistakes, but as far as possible, let what you do or say be dependable—something that a family can rely on with complete assurance that you and the firm you represent can be trusted, that your word is your bond, and that the service you render is dependable.

WANTED: THOSE WHO CAN CARRY OUT INSTRUCTIONS

It seems perfectly clear why we are more valuable and more deserving if we are able to handle *all* funeral and death instructions dependably and without constant supervision. It is human nature to resent being "bossed." Yet, there should be no need for our having to be bossed. When we successfully demonstrate our dependability, we find that the boss is only too glad not to have to do any bossing.

A former president of the National Selected Morticians (NSM) told me this story: When he was a youth, he was just as self-confident, independent of advice, and cocky as the rest of the self-reliant youngsters of his neighborhood. Somewhere along the road to outstanding success, he changed due to the mentorship of an older funeral director who taught him to never be unreliable. When this man was presented the gavel as head of a very prestigious funeral service organization, he was not lauded for his glamour or because he possessed a dynamic personality, or even as a great funeral director. The executive director of NSM praised him in the highest terms as a co-worker for funeral service, who understood how to receive and give instructions, who took other people's suggestions and advice, and who tried to cooperate and compromise at all times no matter what personal inconvenience it might cause.

This great funeral director not only took orders, he carried them out. Gravedigger, sexton, staff, pastor, and families—everyone who worked with him knew he could be depended upon to put it over every time. As a result, new funeral directors almost fought to work for this man because they knew it was a formula for success.

A "LEANER" IS ADMIRED BY NONE

The more dependable and resourceful we are, the more respect we command and deserve from our superiors and fellow employees alike. Unfortunately, most people are "leaners"—always leaning on someone else.

"Why are they sending Eisenhower to Europe for D-Day instead of MacArthur, Bradley, or Patton?" was a great question in this country in the final days of World War II. General MacArthur was famed as a brilliant soldier and had a great record. General Eisenhower was not so famed, possibly not so great a genius.

The answer was made by President Roosevelt, who said simply, "I'll sleep better with Ike over there." He implied that he felt he could depend more upon sturdy Ike than brilliant and flamboyant MacArthur.

THINK FOR YOURSELF

No one can advance with the drawback of undependability dragging at a reputation. When you come right down to it, who deserves to have the chance—the leaner who is always depending on the judgment and action of someone else, or the sturdy character who shoulders responsibility and carries through in a dependable manner?

There is no magic, no secret, no formula for being dependable. The way to be dependable is to be dependable!

DISCUSSION QUESTIONS

1. Give examples of the importance of dependability in general living.

2. How have you been negatively affected in the past by inaccurate information?

3. How do you think is the best way to carry out family instructions?

4. How do you view yourself—as a "leaner" or as being "dependable"?

THE FUNERAL
HOME'S PERSONALITY

"If you would create something, you must be something."
Johann Wolfgang von Goethe

LEARNING OBJECTIVES

- Define the term *Feng Shui.*
- Elaborate on the meaning of *Feng Shui.*
- Identify and label what *personality* is made of.
- Know the meaning of the phrase *exceed expectations.*

DOES YOUR FIRM ATTRACT OR REPEL?

Everyone in funeral service has had the experience of walking into a mortuary or cemetery in a new town and being immediately repelled or attracted by its "personality."

Every funeral home or cemetery has a distinct personality of its own. Sometimes, it is warm, strong, and vital. Sometimes, unfortunately, it is cold and repellent. Many times, it is just lukewarm, wishy-washy, and shallow.

The Chinese have a name for this strange quality which either attracts or repels. For centuries, they have said that every house of business has an individual personality, it's "Feng Shui," as they call it. As crazy as it sounds, a building seems to be able to pick up the personality of its occupants. You can feel it! A young funeral director I knew many years ago took me to look at his first property that he planned to turn into a funeral home. After we walked through the place, he turned to me and said, "This house feels right. It is not cold; it is warm, and I think my families will like it here."

TO OUR FAMILIES, OUR PERSONALITY IS VITAL

It is strange that although a firm's personality is not something we can see with our eyes, it is a definite, tangible *something* that we can and do feel with our heads and our hearts.

What makes up this invisible, yet powerful force? *Your firm's personality is made up of your own and the personalities of everyone engaged in the funeral and remembrance profession.*

Therefore, the power and attractiveness of your firm's personality depends entirely upon you and every individual!

THE DOVE IS MORE ATTRACTIVE THAN THE HAWK

There is a sizable cemetery in the Midwest that is owned by a woman with an attractive personality. She sets the standards of a warm welcome and a warm attitude of cheerful and helpful service, which everyone imitates.

Every cemetery employee simply radiates friendliness and good nature. Waiting on families is a focused passion. They almost smother a person with service, and they do it with sincerity and good feelings.

PERSONALITY EQUALS INCREASED SUCCESS

A highly successful funeral director in Canada gave all his embalming-chemical business to one firm. When asked why he didn't spread it around, he said, "I really don't know. I guess it's because they always seem so glad to hear from me!" If that seems like an overly simple answer, just pause and reflect on how few businesses with whom you deal actually "seem glad" to see you or hear from you.

FAMILIES GO WHERE THEY ARE APPRECIATED

This is a primary quality of a funeral home's personality and one that exerts a great appeal to families. Experiment for yourself with the attitude of sincerely being glad to see your clients, and notice how quickly they respond.

A mortuary science professor purchased practically all his classroom books from one publisher. One day, as he was placing another large order for books, he wrote this publisher, "In 35 years, I have never been in your office. But, from the warm and courteous treatment you have always accorded me, I feel sure that at the door of your offices must be a mat with a large 'WELCOME' appearing and that everyone who crosses your threshold would feel as though they were among old friends."

Thus, through letters and courteous service alone, this firm had impressed its friendly personality upon this busy, unseen client.

Any one individual in an organization can radiate cordiality and warmth for the entire personnel, but no individual can carry the burden alone. Unfortunately, any one individual can cast a light on the firm's personality by a cold, indifferent, negative attitude as well.

The people in any funeral home have a right to be indignant with any member who does not present the best possible front for their firm's personality. This is a responsibility that we should divide and sustain equally.

THE IMPORTANCE OF PUTTING FAMILIES AT EASE

Most individuals who work in funeral service are chosen largely for their ability to impress the community of clients with the attractive personality of the firm they represent. They aim to put the customer absolutely at ease with a warm, courteous, and practically confidential attitude, which makes them feel that they are most welcome and that everything possible will be done to give them the best service and exceed expectations.

Make your firm's personality your personal responsibility. This is partly how success is built!

 DISCUSSION QUESTIONS

1. What can you do to attract people to your funeral home?

2. When and where have you encountered Feng Shui?

3. Describe how you feel when you are treated with appreciation.

4. Why do you think it is important to appreciate each family we serve?

7

CLUES TO SERVING THE FAMILY

"A happy family is but an earlier heaven."

Sir John Bowring

LEARNING OBJECTIVES

- Improve your skills at recognizing the clues to service that families give.

- Identify the danger of judging people.

- Focus on the value of a charitable and tolerant attitude.

- Improve your expertise in understanding the issue of funeral economics.

TRAITS

As funeral professionals, we grow more expert in getting along with others, particularly with families, in direct proportion to our ability to analyze the character of each individual. This ability results in a more complete understanding of their likes and dislikes, their desires and tastes. It can be of great value to you.

We must be alert to catch every clue—by tone of voice, by attitude, by gesture, by action—that will enable us to have a sympathetic understanding of a family and serve them in a way that will win their respect and confidence.

LOOK FOR CLUES TO SERVE THE FAMILY

A couple wanted to pick out a cemetery in which to buy lots and went to a funeral director to take a tour of the various cemeteries in the community. As they entered the funeral director's car, the wife was talking about how she loved flowers and really enjoyed her garden. The funeral director caught the clue instantly.

At first, the funeral director was intending to take the couple to a very contemporary cemetery, but acting on this one clue, he turned the car in the direction of another cemetery known far and wide for its horticultural excellence.

At the gate of the cemetery, he stopped the car and said, "There are several cemeteries around our city, but this one is known as an arboretum." He then drove the couple through the cemetery grounds, noting how neatly the property was landscaped and particularly drawing attention to the magnificent floral gardens throughout.

The couple was enchanted and decided right on the spot that they needed to look no further. Because of one clue that the funeral director picked up, this couple received competent, time-saving service.

WHAT OTHERS EXPECT

As professional people, we should realize that surface indications are seldom to be trusted. It is a mistake to judge the other person by some act or mannerism that may not click with us. When we mentally begin to put "thumbs down" on the other individual, they sense it by some subtle tip-off on our part, and we may have seriously impaired friendly relations.

As funeral directors, the numerous and various people that we meet for the first time put us through a researching analysis mentally, just as we do them. The families are also looking for clues in our actions and work that will tell them whether we are reliable, kindly, honest, and desirable to deal with. Families always mentally appraise us for the advantage they may gain in dealing with us.

SHE CAUGHT THE CLUE

A charitable, tolerant attitude on our part toward others will help families to be attracted to us. A funeral home receptionist in Cincinnati exemplified this virtue—being charitable and gracious to families and the public in spite of negative surface indications that make them seemingly undesirable to deal with. Scowling, an elderly man approached the receptionist and rasped out the name of the deceased person he wanted to see. In a flash, she caught a clue. Waiting on him, she said soothingly, "This cool, damp weather makes my arthritis act up, and it can be a real pain." His gruffness suddenly left him. He smiled and asked in a much milder tone, "How did you know I have been suffering with arthritis? I haven't had a single night's sleep for days." She replied, "I noticed your eyes looked tired from the pain, just as mine do. I really can sympathize with you." The old grump in turn made a sympathetic reply. He wasn't a bear; he just had a jaw ache!

Each family we contact has good points, and we will derive pleasure and advantage by thinking kindly of the other person and treating him or her considerately and tolerantly.

CLUES IN FUNERAL ECONOMICS

In spite of the fact that quality offerings have to cost more than the mediocre or cheap, families sometimes shy away from what they call high prices. A funeral director from Tulsa has a system of identifying and handling these clients. He says, "A larger percentage of our families come in here looking for bargains and that's all right. Sure, I always have a few families who request the best, but if we sold only to them I would not stay in business very long. My system with the price-bargaining client is to ignore the subject of price entirely. I show them everything, from our finest items to our least finest items, and treat them as if they are funeral experts. Eventually, most of them forget the exclusive focus in price and desire real quality. More than 98 percent of my funeral sales are based on quality alone."

His system represents character reading and service offerings of the highest order. Each of us in this great profession can benefit by studying the clues our families send us. It makes for a much healthier relationship and helps create lasting loyalty to your funeral home.

DISCUSSION QUESTIONS

1. What traits do you look for in other people to understand their attitudes?

2. What type of clues do you give to express a mood or feeling?

3. Do you find it easy to read other people's clues?

4. Give an example of when you felt greater understanding of another by reading their clues.

I I

THE WINNING
PROFESSIONAL
ATTITUDE

"Man's actions are the picture book of his creeds."

Ralph Waldo Emerson

SELL THE FUNERAL HOME

"We are not endeavoring to get ahead of others, but to
surpass ourselves."
Hugh B. Brown

LEARNING OBJECTIVES

- Understand that you are a part of the whole.
- Appreciate that the funeral home is the power behind the individual.
- Focus on what truly counts most—*performance.*
- Identify how complimenting the funeral home pays you dividends.

I once was employed by a funeral director whom I observed one day being complimented by a bereaved family. The family was totally satisfied with the service, and they were particularly complimentary about the appearance of the deceased.

The funeral director listened attentively and then responded, "Yes, we have wonderful people associated with the funeral home. I did not do the embalming, or set up the flowers, or even take care of the autos. No, I did not do that, but let me take a minute to introduce you to some of the people who did."

At that point, he motioned for me (I did the embalming) and another associate (who set up the flowers) to come in the chapel.

"Here are the two fine young men you need to compliment. They did most of the work." It was one of the proudest moments of my life, and I will never forget the generosity and wisdom of that veteran funeral director.

In funeral service, this attitude is known as "selling the funeral home," as compared to "selling myself." This veteran funeral director was himself an important part of the funeral home, but he made certain that the client of his business knew that he was simply a part of the whole.

COMPLIMENTING ONE'S FUNERAL HOME COMPLIMENTS ONESELF

Here is a point about selling the funeral home that all of us should grasp: When you praise your funeral home—its staff, service, and ideas—your listener thinks, "You must be capable yourself to appreciate its excellence. You must be an efficient part of an efficient organization."

Funeral service practitioners who have harsh words for their funeral home casts a reflection on their own loyalty. It suggests that they would probably knock any funeral home with which they are associated. It is like a sailor scuttling his or her own ship.

What makes a fine funeral home? Group work! Team work! How strange that everyone can see (except the individual who does it) that those who set themselves up as more important than the company show themselves as ridiculous. Clients and fellow funeral practitioners alike resent any attitude of self-importance, giving the impression that one is "too big for one's job."

THE FUNERAL HOME IS THE POWER BEHIND THE INDIVIDUAL

People who glorify themselves, without giving the funeral home or anyone else connected with it credit for their progress, are riding for a fall. An individual who had purchased a pre-need plan from a funeral director tells the story of how the funeral director tried to sell himself instead of the funeral home.

The funeral director had sold the pre-need service in a very positive fashion, and the client was very satisfied with how things had been handled.

Three years later, this funeral director joined another funeral home. The funeral director quickly called on the pre-need client, saying that the funeral home he now was associated with was nicer, larger, and more beautiful than his former employer. In fact, he went on to explain, the former funeral home had really never appreciated him and the new funeral home did. They had given him more money and authority. "Believe me," the funeral director wound up, "I'm all set up to bring my new employer some new pre-needs, and I'd like to start by moving your funds."

PERFORMANCE IS WHAT COUNTS

The funeral director came off his high horse like a sack of lead as the pre-need client said quietly, "The decision has been made to remain with your former funeral home. This decision is based on the performance and excellence of the funeral home, not on personality alone."

The funeral director had forgotten that it was the quality and service rendered by the funeral home as a whole that established its reputation through which its pre-need and at-need sales were really made. It was the funeral home as a whole, not one individual, that produced the goods and services that were appreciated by clients.

IT IS TO YOUR ADVANTAGE TO "SELL YOUR FUNERAL HOME"

No matter who you are—manager, owner, funeral director/embalmer, apprentice, receptionist—it is to your personal advantage to show genuine enthusiasm for your funeral home—to sell it every chance you get. It makes your funeral home and your work a vital part of your life. Visualize the service your funeral home renders, what it means to your community, and what it means to the comfort and security of so many.

As a sentinel, protecting your funeral home against slurs (arriving from lack of understanding of the great work it is doing), your loyalty will be recognized. You become an inspiration to others. Your attitude not only stimulates you to greater efforts, but inspires your associates to better teamwork. A spirit of boosting is contagious and unleashes a tremendous force to attract more business. That helps everyone in your organization, including you!

YOU SELL YOURSELF WHEN YOU SELL YOUR FUNERAL HOME

When you sell your funeral home, your lack of egotism is pleasing to your clients. The clients think, "This must be a fine funeral home if its employees praise it." The instant you have a good word to say for your funeral home, you radiate enthusiasm that smooths the way for you.

When you "sell the funeral home," you advance its business and *you* advance with it.

DISCUSSION QUESTIONS

1. How can we best sell our funeral home?

2. Do we take the time to compliment each other?

3. Where can the feeling of self-importance lead?

4. What goals in this area can we set for today?

9

CLIENT APPRECIATION

"Life is not so short but there is always time enough for courtesy."

Ralph Waldo Emerson

LEARNING OBJECTIVES

- Identify the dangers of indifference to people.
- Understand the process of satisfying families.
- Know how being tactful helps build character.
- Appreciate that the family is the foundation stone of every funeral home.

MAKE THE CLIENT FEEL IMPORTANT

Everyone who works for a living, whether the head of a company or a rookie, realizes basically that if it were not for customers and clients, *we would not have a job!*

In funeral service, we know that we have to treat our clients with courtesy and decency, or they can, and will, take their service needs elsewhere. After all, there are thousands of funeral homes in Canada and the United States, and that means that a client who calls us actually has many other possible choices. In the funeral home, we know that even the work of personnel who never contact clients directly has a tremendous bearing on the client's satisfaction or dissatisfaction. The reality of all employment is that behind every paycheck is the necessity of pleasing our clients.

All of the men and women who deal with us are more interested in themselves than anyone else in the world! Everyone we serve has a distinct personality and wants to be treated as such. They want you to show appreciation that they selected your funeral home.

This matter of making clients feel important is an essential part of our obligation to humanity to treat others with consideration. We can be assured that they, in turn, will treat *us* with consideration. That mutual exchange of goodwill significantly affects our program; it is the classic win–win situation.

AS A CLIENT, HOW DO YOU REACT?

One way to get along with clients is by showing helpful interest in their problems, creative ways to solve problems, and an alert willingness to be of service. Simply put yourself in the other person's place! What is your reaction when an individual treats you with less attention and respect than you think you deserve?

As funeral directors, we are often the clients. Have you ever gone into a place of business and felt such an attitude of inattention toward you that you have turned around and walked out? Have you ever started to deal with some person who appeared so indifferent about serving you that you either stopped negotiations on the spot or made up your mind to go through with it this time, but never again?

NO ROOM FOR INDIFFERENCE

I once knew a successful funeral director who, from the beginning to the end of his long and active career, made a study of his clients. Daily, this funeral director made the complete rounds of his funeral home, keeping in touch personally with clients and personnel, hearing complaints, taking the trouble to anticipate wants, and always making the customer feel important. In his funeral home, there was no room for indifference.

ATTENTION CREATES OBLIGATIONS

We all have many choices in life. We freely choose where to buy food, where to deposit our money, where to go to school, and what kinds of clothes to wear. No one forces a client to select this or that funeral home. It is a free choice.

What we usually do in selecting our different places to patronize is to respond to and be attracted to the place that gives us the most attention. The business that offers the client the greatest attention is the business that has the greatest chance of establishing a feeling of obligation to the business from the client. This is not manipulation, it is just good sense. All people crave attention, and when they get it, loyalties are established.

The funeral home that sets out to create friends in a structured and organized manner is the firm that is positioning itself today to reap the rewards of client loyalty tomorrow.

BY SATISFYING CLIENTS, WE SATISFY OURSELVES

We experience a keen feeling of pleasure when we know we are doing efficient work. Regardless of its nature, it constitutes a link in the chain of perfect service that satisfies clients. Such work on the part of everyone in the funeral home proves, more than words, that the funeral home is on the job to serve clients and that it is continually striving to earn its clients' loyalty.

In interactions with your clients and associates, you individually can help in the general cause of harmony and efficiency by making them feel important. By your suggestions and examples, others about you will be on their toes to convince every client that his or her funeral home choice is justified, valued, and appreciated. Your personality becomes more attractive to everyone as you cultivate the habit of making others feel important.

TRY TO TREAT EVERYONE ALIKE

The following experience, as observed by an eyewitness, illustrates the wisdom of showing by our attitude that *every* client is important. One never knows just what possibilities any client really possesses.

An elderly man, clad in rough clothing, walked into a jewelry store in a Midwestern town. Several days' growth of beard covered his rugged face. The salesperson who greeted him was a woman who was as friendly toward the old man as if he had been dressed like a nobleman. She said, in response to his inquiry concerning a woman's watch, "Do you wish to see something in a jeweled case like I'm wearing?" In response to his murmured reply, she displayed half a dozen platinum and diamond-cased watches on the velvet pad on the counter.

Presently, she was placing his purchase—a delicate, gleaming, diamond watch—in a satin-lined case. The old man was beaming. As he left, he said to the proprietor, "This is a nice place. I've been to two other stores, but I don't think they liked me. The lady here shows you what you want right away without any foolin' around." The old man's "shopping" amounted to $3,000 for that watch!

TACT BUILDS CONFIDENCE

You see the point: The saleswoman dignified the old man. She did not say, "What price do you want to pay?" Oh, no. She offered to show him the jeweled cases first. Then, she gave him a graceful, easy "out" by adding, "Or do you prefer just the plain, gold case?," thus making it a matter of his preference rather than of his pocketbook.

A younger salesperson in the store said to the older one, "How did you know he had any money?" The latter replied, with sincerity: "I didn't know. I never know how much money *anyone* has who walks in here, but I try to treat everyone as though he were going to buy a $2,000 diamond."

As it turned out, the elderly customer owned one of the best farms in the state and went shopping at that jewelry store again to the tune of more than $11,000!

You see, you can never tell how many possibilities a person that you are serving may have. The important thing is what the right attitude does for you and your funeral home. The right motive makes you a pleasing person to deal with, adds charm to your personality, and puts you in line for the blessings that fate holds for those whose heart is in the right place. If a career in the funeral service profession is anything, it is a matter of the heart.

QUALITY

The only safe rule is to build up, dignify, and put on a pedestal every client of your funeral home with whom you have contact. Some of those you dignify may not deserve it, and some may make it very difficult on you, but every time you practice it, you will advance yourself in the fine art of being a helpful, sincere, genuine person—a person of quality.

Harry S Truman once asked a bellman in front of a hotel what kind of people were easiest to get along with. "The quality person," answered the bellman, "always the quality, Mr. Truman."

When you treat people as "quality," their reaction to you and your organization is bound to be of a far higher quality than with any other human relations approach. You can bet that the funeral home down the street is not practicing the same level of quality treatment.

Clients are the foundation stones of every funeral home. They provide your job and other jobs, making it possible for your funeral home and you to prosper. Clients stay where the service proves their patronage is appreciated. Whatever your job, do your part in ensuring client appreciation.

 DISCUSSION QUESTIONS

1. When you are a client, what do you expect?

2. What happens when you truly appreciate your clients? (Give examples.)

3. How do we satisfy ourselves by satisfying clients?

4. What role does tact play?

10

ENTHUSIASM

"I never did a day's work in my life—it was all fun."

Thomas A. Edison

 LEARNING OBJECTIVES

- Understand why keeping your imagination working is important.

- Appreciate the idea that every day is a new opportunity to serve.

- Identify, label, and elaborate on the one great goal in funeral service—family satisfaction.

- Explain why every person should receive enthusiastic service.

ENTHUSIASM IS CONTAGIOUS

Nothing is more contagious than enthusiasm except the lack of it!

A stage play running in New York is now in its fourth year, and audiences continue to get excited over it. There is only one member left of the original cast, but she is as enthusiastic over the play and her lines as when she started to enact her role over three years ago. She has unquenchable, unbeatable enthusiasm.

The ex-members of the cast simply ran out of steam and enthusiasm for their work. Their acting became lifeless and uninspiring. Repeating the same words without a change, night after night, became deadly monotonous.

WHEN THEY LOST OUT

They lost enthusiasm because they ran out of imagination. They became too self-centered to observe things that would have kept their interest alive. The audience was continually new and deserved to hear the lines as though they were being spoken for the first time. People came to see and hear what they might reasonably expect would give them a never-to-be-forgotten experience and inspiration. Every member of the cast had a glorious opportunity to create an enduring impression.

More earnest thinking about the clients and less about the grind could have given new force and meaning to the work of those who failed and left the cast. With imagination gone, they lost enthusiasm and degenerated into mere talking machines and so lost their places in the big show.

KEEP YOUR IMAGINATION WORKING

Funeral service can often degenerate into what has just been described.

Many funeral directors on the "stage" begin a career ambitiously. They speak and act with enthusiasm and point their efforts zealously toward advancement. Then, encountering the many obstacles that challenge their courage, self-esteem, and skill, they become discouraged. They become blind to the human interests around them—blind to the possibilities on every hand to perform quality funeral service that has a proven history of winning business, friends, and advancement.

The routine work of funeral service may be an old story to you. However, what may be routine to you is the only funeral that a family will ever have for this significant person. Your work in funeral service, whatever it is, must be of such quality that clients, directly or indirectly affected by it, will be sold every time on the excellent service your funeral home renders. A funeral home's reputation for service (as with an individual) must be recreated today and every day.

IT IS NEW EACH DAY

It is hard for enthusiasm to run down when your imagination is on the upbeat. Visualize your work from the viewpoint of an outsider, as though you were just tackling it for the first time. It has possibilities that you have never considered. Visualize the service your funeral home performs and its role in the great life drama of your community. You will quickly see that caretaking of the dead and caregiving to the living are indispensable community services. In other words, what a mess we would be in without funeral directors! See your work with new eyes, tackle it with fresh energy, and others will respond to your enthusiasm.

MAGNIFICENT ENTHUSIASM

Winston Churchill, the great English statesman, once saw a Hindu workman hoisting bushel sacks of coal onto freight cars in India. Churchill was fascinated by the vigor with which the man tackled each sack, threw it up on his shoulders, ran up a short gangplank, and deposited it with a flourish in just the right spot among the other bags so as to save space and, thus, load the car more efficiently.

Speaking to the man, Churchill said, "You work with great enthusiasm!" The workman, startled that the famous man was speaking to him, smiled widely and replied, "Sir, it is always different and I use my imagination to keep it from being monotonous. It is a game. Each sack of coal is a new enemy to conquer. I see how many enemies I can conquer and I make records and then I beat them. You see, I have children to feed. I feed them by being triumphant over my imaginary enemy!"

Churchill applauded the man for his creativity and later said the experience was worth a month's pay. With such magnificent enthusiasm, we can accomplish wonders in our funeral homes.

THE GOAL

Our great goal in funeral service is one thing: client satisfaction. Our progress hinges upon it! *Your work* is an important link in the chain of service that wins repeat clients even though you may not directly see the client. Keeping that reality in focus and your imagination alive to this fact will help sustain your enthusiasm.

THE CLIENT COULD BE A PRIME MINISTER!

Everyone we meet in our funeral home is immediately, if sometimes subconsciously, aware of our enthusiasm or our lack of it. We never know just how important a contact may be.

When the first cartridge fountain pens were introduced, R. B. Bennett, the former Prime Minister of Canada, read an advertisement about them and concluded they would make ideal Christmas gifts. He was so enthusiastic about his idea that he postponed an important meeting to go in person to the leading stationery shop in his city.

A young salesman greeted Bennett with scarcely polite civility, not recognizing him, of course. Disregarding this cold reception because he was warmed with his own enthusiasm, the Prime Minister stated his desire to have one hundred pens in solid gold, and one hundred in sterling silver, each to be engraved with the Canadian coat of arms and the name of the recipient. The order meant thousands of dollars.

The young man merely stared blankly and said, "Oh, those pens. Let me see, I don't think we have enough for that kind of order. Anyway, I don't think they work."

The Prime Minister's first impulse was to walk out. Then, he leaned over the counter looking straight into the salesman's eyes, and said, "Will you kindly tell the proprietor that the Prime Minister of Canada desires to see him at once!"

The salesman turned pale.

THE WAY OF INDIFFERENCE IS HARD

The proprietor of the stationery store came running. Then, Bennett gave the salesman a scathing lecture on courtesy, and the proprietor of the store discharged the salesman on the spot. The distinguished Prime Minister, however, was a man known far and wide for his kindness. Now, with his indignation appeased, he pleaded for the young man's reinstatement, placed his big order with the shop, and left with a smile.

Having learned the hard lesson of what a lack of enthusiasm can do, that young salesman doubtless became the most alert and attentive person in the place, no matter who he served.

IT BRINGS SUCCESS SOON

Our work in each of our funeral homes today is an integral part of our future. Therefore, each day of enthusiastic attention to our duties as funeral professionals brings us closer to successful achievements.

Enthusiasm is the bridge that will carry you from small accomplishments to great ones!

DISCUSSION QUESTIONS

1. How can we sustain our enthusiasm levels, year after year?

2. What can we learn from the prime minister story?

3. How much enthusiasm is too much?

4. How can we help each other generate day-to-day enthusiasm?

11

"SO WHAT?"

"It is no use saying 'We are doing our best.' You have got to succeed in doing what is necessary."

Sir Winston Churchill

 LEARNING OBJECTIVES

- Explain how this attitude is the wrong way to impress.

- Understand and explain why families respond to sincere concern.

- Understand the domino effect of "so what?."

- Explain the relationships between artificial nonchalance and "so whatting."

THE WRONG WAY FOR A FUNERAL PROFESSIONAL TO IMPRESS

We live in very fast times. We have invented things to make life exciting—cross-continent trips, computers, medical marvels, and special movie effects—which come along so quickly that they cease to be miracles and become yawns.

The swift pace has done things to people. It has prematurely aged minds and dulled enthusiasm. One tragic result of a tired-of-it-all, worldly wise attitude is that it revolves itself into the parrot-like intonation, "so what?," about anything that might reasonably be expected to arouse interest.

The "so what?" attitude has a paralyzing effect on personality, and particularly in the funeral home. The funeral professional so afflicted is a "pain in the neck" to everyone that he or she contacts.

AS POISONOUS AS A RATTLESNAKE

The phrase, "so what?," born as a smart-aleck saying, actually represents an *attitude of mind!* It is as poisonous to successful human relationships as a den of rattlesnakes.

The truth is that the "so whatters" only betray ignorance by their attitude. They think they are wise, blasé, and nonchalant, but are they? Put to the test, you will find them shallower than a saucer. When this attitude engulfs those contacting the funeral public, they become like lost souls, until they snap out of it and realize their mistake.

HIS MISTAKE

A leading Philadelphia funeral firm took in a young apprentice funeral director who had graduated at the top of his mortuary science college class. This young man showed great dedication, and he had formed a strong relationship with a monument company within the first month. This relationship was bringing extra money to the firm, and the senior funeral directors were very impressed.

Within months, older members of the funeral firm noted a striking change in the apprentice. His association with this outstanding funeral firm seemed to have gone to his head. He became cocky, and his standard phrase was "so what?."

Soon, he was no longer invited into the confidences of the funeral home. At the end of his first year, the other funeral directors were dumbfounded to learn that the monument company had dumped the funeral home, and the apprentice had failed his state law exam and was ineligible for final licensure.

The root of the mess was that the apprentice had been "so whatting" both the monument company and the State Board of Funeral Directors and Embalmers.

The senior funeral director called the worldly wise young apprentice into his office, expecting to find him broken in spirit due to his failure. When he mentioned the loss of the monument business and the failure of the board, however, the answer he received was "so what?."

"I'll tell you WHAT," barked the funeral director, "you are no longer a member of this firm—THAT'S WHAT!"

FAMILIES RESPOND TO ENTHUSIASM

Let us look at the direct opposite of the "so what?" attitude. A funeral professional with wholesome curiosity in seeing what makes the world tick is almost invariably friendly, human, and interesting.

A funeral receptionist had a widow in the office of the funeral home. The widow wanted more acknowledgment cards, but she also just wanted to talk. The receptionist was swamped with paperwork and said to the widow: "I'm not your funeral director. They're all out at a service, but I can help you if you wish."

The widow was more than anxious to let this person help her, but what she really wanted was just to sit and talk. After two hours, the funeral director returned. The widow was still in the office but was preparing to leave. As she left, she looked at the funeral director and said, "I can't praise your receptionist enough. She is so full of enthusiasm to help. She is a real gem. Hold on to her!"

FROGS IN THE FUNERAL POND

"So whatters," on the other hand, sink into an issue of their own making—the murky quicksand of artificial nonchalance. Around the border of the mental swamp of stagnation sit the bloated frogs of lost hope. Night and day, they croak over and over the words, "so what?."

If we, as funeral professionals, are to win friends and families and advance our own interests of the funeral home where we work, we must forever resist the phrase and the attitude of "so what?." To adopt it is to lose. An inquiring, enthusiastic point of view invites the best that other people can give.

 DISCUSSION QUESTIONS

1. How can we save ourselves from the "so whatter" and help each other stay positive?

2. What is the opposite of the "so what" attitude?

3. When you adopt the positive attitude, what are the results?

4. Think of an instance where you may have slipped into "so what"; what were the consequences, and how did you handle them?

12
STAND BY YOUR WORD

"No man has a good enough memory to be a successful liar."
Abraham Lincoln

LEARNING OBJECTIVES

- Be able to explain the importance of promise keeping.
- Explain ways to make your word good.
- Explain how unkept promises undermine confidences.
- Appreciate how promises and family satisfaction go together.

THE TOUGH CANADIAN

This story happened years ago when Sir Robert Laird Borden was the Prime Minister of Canada.

In the unexplored, lifeless land beyond the Arctic Circle, the Eskimos had experienced a growing food shortage as wildlife in that region had diminished. The Canadian government, out of sheer generosity, was determined to send a herd of 5,000 reindeer to that area as a food source. The herd would have to be gathered at Aklawik, Alaska, 2,000 miles from the proposed base at the delta of the MacKenzie River. Canadian authorities were advised that the man for the job of moving the herd was Andrew Bahr, a Laplander guide who knew his way around the land of ice and snow with his eyes shut.

Bahr accepted the job of driving the vast herd of reindeer to starving Eskimos 2,000 miles away, and Robert Borden hoped that the right man had been chosen.

With three trusted helpers, Andy began a tremendous trek that is an unparalleled saga in suffering, hardship, and obstacles. Time and again his herd stampeded, and hundreds of reindeer after nine months perished from fatigue and in fording hazardous rivers. Disaster in various forms threatened the expedition. Only a man of Bahr's iron nerve and indomitable will could have resisted the impulse to quit cold. He completed his job, reaching the delta of the MacKenzie with 3,000 reindeer, most of which were the offspring of the original herd. It was a story unparalleled in Canadian history and when the press asked Prime Minister Borden his opinion of Bahr and the operation, Borden simply replied, "Andy kept his promise."

BE SURE YOU CAN KEEP A PROMISE

As funeral professionals, whether we are driving "herd," directing a funeral, or managing a cemetery, there is one dependable rule that will enable us to keep our promises: Never make promises you are not sure can be kept! We all want to please and accommodate; nevertheless, this rule is the only safe way.

I once worked for a funeral director who purchased a new ambulance. My boss was very concerned about having enough oxygen for long trips because we were a rural funeral home. The manager of the ambulance's sales office assured him, "You have enough oxygen for a two-hour trip." "Are you sure?" my boss asked. "You have my word on it," the sales manager replied.

You guessed it. On our first long run, we ran out of oxygen within 40 minutes. My boss was furious. He stalked into the sales manager's office and said, "That ambulance of yours is out there on the street. The deal's off. I don't want it or any other of your ambulances. Give me my money back right now! I'll only buy where people keep their promises."

Eventually, the problem was solved, but the point is this: The salesman made a promise that could not be kept.

MAKE YOUR WORD GOOD

Whenever someone depends on your promise to work well, be sure you know you can fulfill that promise. If you are *not* sure, you can always check with someone who is. You might have to go to the manager of the funeral home, but it is always worth the trouble.

A successful Chicago pre-need salesperson was talking to a family concerning a large funeral policy. During the conversation, a family member asked, "Can I cash this in later, or can I use this if I move?" The pre-need salesperson frankly didn't know. She risked the chance of losing the sale by admitting it. "But," she added, "I can let you know in five minutes." The family member smiled and said, "I can wait five minutes for anyone honest enough not to make promises that they are not sure can be backed up." As it turned out, the policy they had been talking about did not fill the prospect's demands. The family did buy another one that did, from this candid young woman, before the afternoon was over.

UNKEPT PROMISES UNDERMINE CONFIDENCES

In funeral service, there are innumerable examples of the necessity of not making promises of which we are unsure. For example, when a family asks you if you will be there to conduct the funeral, it is because they want to share their experience with you, and to have the confidence that it will be done right. If you say yes, and then don't appear—well?

You get the point: Keeping promises in the funeral profession is more important and magnified because you cannot go back and remedy the unkept promise. If you do not show up for the funeral appointment, you cannot do it over again.

The gravest danger of unkept promises is that they not only injure us but also the funeral home we represent. They actually endanger the funeral home's future. As funeral professionals, we are in the business to make friends (not enemies) for ourselves and our firm.

KEEP FAITH WITH YOUR FAMILIES

To avoid breaking your promise, there are three general *Do nots:*

1. Do not promise any service or performance that you are not absolutely sure can be delivered.
2. Do not make a guarantee that you are not sure can be fulfilled.
3. Do not make vague or shaky promises.

Your families will think more of you and your funeral home if you do not make idle promises. In the funeral profession or anywhere else, no one has any admiration for the person who promises and then falls down on his word.

DISCUSSION QUESTIONS

1. What situations come up in which families want promises that may be hard to fulfill?

2. Why is it so important to promise only what you absolutely can deliver?

3. Where do you personally need more business knowledge so that you know the extent of the promises that can be made?

4. Share any stories about unkept promises.

13

PROFESSIONAL ARROGANCE

"Life is a long lesson of humility."

Sir James M. Barrie

 LEARNING OBJECTIVES

- Understand why arrogance is the archenemy of goodwill.

- Be able to explain how a condescending attitude angers families.

- Explain the risk of being arrogant with a family.

- Be able to articulate why there is no substitute for friendliness.

WHAT DOES IT GET THEM?

To people who have the gift of true humility, it is always a mystery as to what arrogant individuals hope to gain by their attitude.

Webster defines arrogance as "a sense of affectation of superiority." Undoubtedly, the haughty "superior" being is trying to impress his or her importance on others. If these people could know the secret discomfort and resentment that is aroused when they constantly try to impress, they would stop their actions immediately.

This type of arrogance is very dangerous in the caring profession of funeral service. Rather than winning respect, such an attitude marks its owner as having an overinflated ego—what psychologists call a "superiority complex." This person's mind is classed as being self-centered and, instead of impressing, merely arouses contempt.

The point of this book is to win as many friends as possible for our funeral homes. The formula for winning friends never changes. Its important elements are sincerity, friendliness, and humility. Far too many people, entrusted with the responsibility of dealing with clients, have the serious and dangerous fault of high-hatting. In the funeral home, this can be fatal and costly. One arrogant staff person can drive away more families than a dozen sensible people can create.

CONDESCENDING ATTITUDES ANGER FAMILIES

Sir Wilfrid Lauier, the great Prime Minister of Canada, once said, "The true gauge of superiority is humility." Great men are invariably humble men. They know so much that they are able to realize how little they know.

A teller in a Boston bank was called on the carpet and told he would have to mend his manners or look for another job. Amazed, he said, "I don't understand, I show our depositors every courtesy." "Oh, you're courteous in your own way," his boss replied, "but you're so confounded condescending about it."

This rebuke followed the complaint of an old fruit dealer. He had told the bank's cashier, "I know my deposits are not very large at times, but I give your bank all my business. What makes me so angry is the way the teller always acts like I'm just depositing peanuts!"

A HIGH HAT IS KNOCKED OFF

You can't get away with arrogance in funeral service forever. "Lording it over" the other fellow is sure failure to a successful career with the public.

The founder, no longer the active leader of a famous Washington, D.C., funeral home, went into the office of the funeral home to get some information one day. The funeral assistant at the desk did not recognize the tall, stooped, Lincolnesque figure. He answered the old funeral director's questions with great disdain, scarcely even looking in the old gentleman's direction.

The old funeral director finally said, "I want to ask just one more question, sir. What is your name?" The young man drew himself up haughtily, saying, "I'm sure I can't understand how that could be of any interest to you." "You'll understand in the morning," said the founder, and stalked out.

That funeral employee got some news the next morning which was very unpleasant, yet well deserved.

THERE IS NO SUBSTITUTE FOR FRIENDLINESS

Some high-hatters, to be sure, get by with it for a time. Don't worry, they don't last forever. The high-hat, arrogant attitude is poison. It is dynamite, as well as ridiculous. It is the direct opposite of what we all know is the successful attitude in dealing with others in funeral service.

Success in handling families calls for warmth, friendliness, and level-headed commonsense. It is a fatal mistake in our profession to be otherwise.

DISCUSSION QUESTIONS

1. Why is professional arrogance so dangerous?

2. What would you do if you observed a condescending attitude in one of your associates?

3. Why will a "high-hatter" never succeed?

4. Give an example of a situation in which the client was arrogant, and tell how you did or how you would handle it.

14

THE FUNERAL PROFESSION REQUIRES TOLERANCE

"Keep cool and you command everybody."

Louis Leon de Saint-Just

LEARNING OBJECTIVES

- Know the definition of a tolerant person.

- Understand what the *mentionable–manageable* motto means.

- Know the tolerant procedures for dealing with mistakes.

- Explain why a funeral director cannot expect every break to be a good one.

IT IS FUN TO GIVE THE OTHER PERSON A BREAK

If the following description of a tolerant person fits you, then you are getting much happiness out of life, you have the faculty of winning friends, and success in this great profession will smile upon your efforts.

A tolerant individual is one who has a sympathetic understanding of another person's beliefs and practices. He or she has an attitude of forbearance toward another person's views, opinions, or actions, although he or she may not be in full accord with them.

INTOLERANCE LOSES FAMILIES

A successful executive in Chicago had used the same funeral home for years. When his aunt died, he once again called the firm, but since his last funeral experience the firm had been sold to a young funeral director.

During the arrangements, the executive had requested that a brief statement be added in the memorial service folder about a reception following the service. When the cards arrived at the funeral home, the executive noticed that the statement inviting people to the funeral reception was absent. He said to the young funeral director, "I guess you didn't hear my request for the reception statements on the cards." The funeral director replied, "Mister, if we had put that on the cards, it would have crowded the printing and would have cost you more." The executive was stunned. "I have the money," he replied. The funeral director was firm. The cards were going to stay the way they were. The executive looked at the young funeral director and said, "I have been a patron of this firm for years, but this is my last time."

Had that young funeral director been more tolerant of that little request from a solid patron and a man who was not ordinarily fussy, a good client would not have been lost. A patient, generous attitude is the only attitude a professional can have toward a family. Just imagine how different that executive's attitude would have been had the funeral director said, "My mistake, sir. I'll correct it immediately," and not only redone the wording on the card, but ordered one hundred more for good measure, and for free!

Here is a suggested motto concerning tolerant, giving service that should be over the front door of every funeral home:

> If it is mentionable by a family, it should be manageable by the funeral home.

SHE LOST OUT BY HER INTOLERANCE

There was a funeral director who managed a funeral home and was really a fine person, very popular, and respected by her staff. One year, the funeral home hit a slump in volume. It was a terrible year, and this manager was frazzled. Eventually, the volume returned and things began to pick up, but the staff noticed a big change in this manager. Whenever something went wrong at the funeral home, the manager would mope and would blame everyone else for any misfortune. She even referred to her staff as a bunch of "dopes." Soon, her developed intolerance of every little bad break became noticeable to the community. Whereas the community had admired this manager before, they were now distant and withdrawn. Within two years, the funeral director was released.

She had lost her tolerance and her generous, friendly nature toward her staff and her community, and the staff and community lost its tolerance of her.

"THUMBS UP" SPIRIT WINS RESPECT

To be tolerant of the appearance of others is a pleasing clue to one's character. To be tolerant of the opinion of others stamps one as a person of kindness. It invites confidence that is seldom offered to one who is too critical and too pushy.

Herbert Hoover once wrote to a friend, "When I judge a man, I sum up his character as a whole, and I always assume he is a good man even when the odds seem tremendously against such a belief." That is a tolerant, broad-ranged view. Too many of us make judgments of people and are too ready to turn "thumbs down" at the slightest indication of some traits of which we do not approve.

TOLERANT DEALINGS WITH MISTAKES

If someone accuses you of a mistake, you will strengthen yourself in that person's estimation by a tolerant attitude. If you are wrong, it will not hurt you to frankly admit it and indicate your willingness to do all you can to make it right. You can say with a smile to your accuser, "Being human, I'm not above making mistakes—speak freely." It will pave the way to a friendly adjustment of the trouble.

If you are right, don't fly up in righteous indignation. It may, in that case, be wise to quietly explain such facts as will convince the other that the mistake is not of your making. In any case, make allowances for the other person's attitude, consider his circumstances, and realize that after he cools down he will regard you with increased respect.

FUNERAL DIRECTOR PROVES BIGGER
THAN HIS CRITICS

A certain funeral director in Florida had a news article written about his funeral home that held his business and his profession up to ridicule. The funeral director had every right to be indignant, as were his friends who knew him to be a "grand person." When a photographer for the same newspaper again came to him for the privilege of photographing him and the operation, the funeral director astonished everyone by his willing cooperation. He later explained his attitude in this way, "As a funeral director, my profession makes me vulnerable to criticism or ridicule, as well as to praise. I can't expect every break to be a good one, and I'm prepared to take the bitter with the sweet."

Tolerance inspires tolerance. When you contact a family, you can figure that some of them will have no particular reason for being patient or tolerant of you. It's their money that they are going to spend, and they might figure you should be the tolerant one.

STUDY FUNERAL PROFESSIONALS THAT YOU ADMIRE

Study funeral directors that you admire. Watch how they deal with families and the public. See for yourself the type of funeral director who attracts friends and is popular with families. You will find tolerance as an outstanding quality in their makeup.

 DISCUSSION QUESTIONS

1. Have you ever seen a funeral professional lose his or her patience?

2. Do you believe that if something is mentionable by a family it should be manageable by the funeral home?

3. Are you tolerant of others' mistakes?

4. Give examples of how you can be more tolerant.

15

PATIENCE IN THE SELECTION ROOM

"Patience is the support of weakness; impatience is the ruin of strength."

Charles Caleb Colton

LEARNING OBJECTIVES

- Define the term *rush act*.

- Explain how to avoid the rush act.

- Explain the potential consequences of impatience.

- Understand the importance of patience.

FAMILIES DEMAND PATIENT SERVICE

The suppliers in the funeral profession have done what amounts to an outstanding job in developing product knowledge, merchandising and marketing strategies, and general presentation skill development. There is no doubt that we have more information pertaining to funeral products today than our ancestors in funeral service ever dreamed possible. With all the great information available, one area that has not received a great amount of attention in the sale of funeral products is old-fashioned patience.

W. F. Cody, the famed western plainsman, writing of the time he and a companion went hunting with the Crow Indians up in the Pryor Mountains of Montana, said, "A true sportsman and hunter doesn't rush into the hunt. No, when he gets into the game country he will go to where the deer feed, and then

sit down in some bushes. He does not run the game out of the country, he sits and waits."

Many of us in funeral service can apply this bit of old-fashioned strategy to our own procedures when presenting caskets, urns, vaults, or any other valuable funeral products to a family. Is there ever a tendency on our part to run our families out of the selection room because we have not developed or exercised the patience necessary in dealing with others? Yet, we demand that the other person show a patient and respectful attitude toward us when the rules are reversed.

DON'T WE LIKE TO TAKE OUR TIME?

There always have been, and probably always will be, many exasperating occurrences in dealing with the public in funeral service. Some of us cannot understand why so many people are so "picky" and why it takes them so long to make up their minds. Yet, when you are making an important decision, or spending your own hard-earned money, don't you want to feel sure you are not making a mistake? Do you want everybody to give you the "rush act"? Probably not. Always keep this in mind: Studies indicate that families who spend more time and are given the time to spend in the selection of funeral products more often than not increase their own investment in such important items. They usually express a greater degree of satisfaction with the funeral home following the service.

A highly successful funeral director in Portland, Maine, relayed the following story about patience in the selection room.

"It is not unusual for our families to take half an hour to an hour to make a casket selection, and we encourage it. It is not unusual to have shown 15 or 20 caskets to a family and have an agreement almost in hand, and then some other member of the family may decide it is not right and we willingly start all over. The purchase of a casket is a once-in-a-lifetime decision and, frankly, we make quite a fuss over the whole thing. We want our clients to experience what the casket is, what it represents, and what benefit is in it for them. We cannot afford to rush or force a decision, which is why all of our funeral directors were given a framed motto to hang in their office, containing only one word—PATIENCE. This is the motto we should all have hanging in the office of our minds.

NO FAMILY LIKES TO BE RUSHED

One hasty word at the wrong time in the selection room can destroy the goodwill you built up in the arrangement conference. It must be remembered that a family has the natural desire to be sure in their minds that every angle of the agreement is entirely to their own liking. A family in Sacramento had a death and called a funeral home they had never used before (they were new to the community). When it came time to purchase an urn, the funeral director took them to the urn display and said, "The prices are clearly marked, and a description of each urn is written on the cards. I'll leave you a minute to make your selection." Exactly one minute later, the funeral director returned. "Have you made your selection yet?" "No, I haven't. What's the rush?" replied the husband. "No rush at all," said the funeral director, "but to tell you the truth, we got extremely busy last night and I do have another family waiting." "Well, I guess you better get upstairs and go ahead with that other family," the husband replied. "Can I use your phone to call another funeral home?"

Are people touchy? You bet! Has loyalty to funeral homes changed? You bet! That funeral director should have done anything and everything, except what he did. He made the family feel insignificant by rushing them. In turn, they rebelled, and rightfully so, and the funeral home lost out. Human nature is like that.

FAMILIES RESENT THE RUSH ACT

Probably the greatest tragedy in the rush act is that more families do not tell us to our faces how they felt hurried or rushed in the selection of merchandise.

A manager who was responsible for 20 locations was checking his list of funeral directors to see how their sale of merchandise was going. At the bottom of the list was a man who had been a ball of fire the first six months of the year and was now looking hopeless. The manager talked it over with him. The funeral director said, "I don't know why I'm in such a slump. Would you watch my casket demonstration and see if you can figure it out?"

The manager agreed and solved the trouble in a couple of demonstrations. It was the old case of the "rush act." The funeral director was so afraid he might say the wrong thing that he zipped his families through the selection room lickety-split! On one occasion, he even told a family that he had another appointment and hoped that 15 minutes would be enough time. Sounds strange? Yes. But what's even more strange, and probably not all that uncommon, is the fact that the funeral director was oblivious to what he was doing.

For whatever reason, he had developed a bad habit in the selection room, and no one knew what the real trouble was. The manager sized up the situation. He slowed the funeral director down from his rush act and soon had him up among the performing funeral professionals.

Funeral directors who come in contact with families sometimes pull the rush act because they are honestly trying to save time. However, we certainly cannot afford to save time at the risk of losing business. Schedule, organize, and pace yourself. We owe it to our families to give them time to feel satisfied that the funeral transaction is entirely to their benefit.

THE RUSH ACT IS A RUSH ACT

Rushing a family, or the failure to allow them enough time to make up their minds, will drive people away and will translate into reduced revenue for the funeral home. Families should never be given any reason to feel that we do not have time to serve them to the best of our ability. All funeral professionals agree with this credo. Guard against any attitude that causes a family to feel you are in a hurry.

If you feel a situation is getting into the "rush act" class—SLOW DOWN! Let the situation coast a little. You will make a great point if everyone sees you as a patient funeral professional.

 DISCUSSION QUESTIONS

1. Give examples of professional patience.

2. Have you ever experienced the "rush act"?

3. How can you help a family slow down?

4. What are some rewards in taking your time?

16

THE FUNERAL HOME GOPHER

"People who think they are too big to do little things are perhaps too little to be asked to do big things."

Author Unknown

 LEARNING OBJECTIVES

- Understand the *real* message of this chapter.
- Appreciate what *bottoms up* means.
- Articulate the positive attitude of the character in this story.
- Understand the relationship between luck and work.

The job at the funeral home was small and offered small pay and long hours, but this woman took it anyway. She said that she was not afraid of work and wanted to learn the funeral profession from the bottom up. Think of that—a person choosing the hard way instead of trying to land the soft job.

She did not seem to have sense enough to see that she was only a cog in a great big machine, that too many were ahead of her for the big jobs and that she would be nuts to kill herself working—because she was the funeral home gopher.

This woman actually believed the fairy tale about people's progress in life being in proportion to their own efforts.

She also missed a lot of fun because she spent her spare time reading and studying anything she could get her hands on about the funeral service profession. Yet, unbelievably, she was always cheerful, seemingly not having sense enough to know that the funeral home would take advantage of her if she were always good natured. In addition, she never seemed to think of her own convenience in dealing with families. She didn't get the idea or realize that the more you do for others, the more they expect.

She certainly was a slow learner. She treated every family as if they were royalty. Someone in the funeral home tried to tip her that since she was the gopher it was foolish to work so hard to please, that families are not as sensitive as she seemed to think and don't know whether a funeral director is breaking his or her neck to serve them, and don't appreciate it anyway! No, the funeral home gopher went right ahead working like a beaver to please every family. She actually acted as though she was part owner of the funeral home.

One could not help liking her. However, she had an irritating way of keeping silent, with a faraway look in her eyes, whenever you knocked anyone to her. She did not spend a lot of time in the employees' coffee room. She actually seemed to like doing funerals. She was so different and odd that she never tried to shift a tough job onto others' shoulders. She tried to whip the problem herself, without leaning on someone else— heroic, but stupid!

She also did not have sense enough to be discriminating. She would make every effort to give a family dependable service no matter who the family might be. It was pitiful the way she needlessly exerted herself to serve people who probably did not appreciate it anyway.

Her prize offense was that whenever she had an idea she was sure was good for the funeral home and would help families, she actually had the nerve to take it to the owner just for the good it might do the business. She did not seem to have the good sense to keep her ideas to herself like everybody else did. Someone tried to wise her up that she was just the gopher and was not getting paid enough as it was (nor were any of the other "slaves," for that matter) and advised her to "let the funeral home take care of its own problems."

The funny thing was that the owner of the funeral home never scolded this woman for butting in. He actually praised her for her cooperation and her creativity. The gopher also seemed to take for granted that others would treat her as well as she treated them. She had a way of saying, "Hold the right thought toward others and they will reciprocate." It seemed that she just could not get down to reality. She always seemed to figure she made her own breaks and somehow she did get good breaks consistently. Just fool's luck.

Whenever someone got a promotion, the gopher never sulked or stalled on the job. She always rejoiced in the other's success. She said the example was good for her, made her work harder, and that by applying the same principles she would advance too.

She surely had weird ideas about working in a funeral home. There never was such a loser! However, she finally lost her job—the owner of the funeral home made her the manager.

DISCUSSION QUESTIONS

1. Have you ever been the gopher in the funeral home?

2. What was the gopher experience like?

3. Discuss why this role is so important.

4. Give examples of how the gopher moved up in the funeral home.

17

APPROVAL

"Reprove thy friend privately; commend him publicly."

Old Saying

LEARNING OBJECTIVES

- Explain why it is normal for everyone to want to be liked.

- Understand that your approval must be real.

- Explain the relationship between approving of people and the attraction of their business.

- Understand and articulate the relationship between criticism and being constructive.

WE HUNGER FOR IT

Most of us do not seem to realize that, like ourselves, every person we contact, families and fellow workers included, enjoys and wants praise—a "pat on the back."

Leonard Bernstein, long-time conductor of the New York Philharmonic and developer of many outstanding musicians, once said, "The most important thing in a conductor's bag of tricks is to know when and how to praise a player."

What Bernstein meant was that a conductor has to know how much approval, what kind, and when to apply it in order to give praise its full buildup of strength. Praise worms out of a person the good that is inside.

That wise statement brings out an important phase of the subject: the *positive* nature of approval. Our expressions of approval, therefore, achieve the very objective we desire most in our contact with others, which is making the other warm up to us and like us.

For years, I have been getting my shoes shined by the same group of people. The owner of the shop calls himself "Dr. Shine" and has a handmade diploma from "Shoe U" hanging over the seat in his shop. The proprietor is an entertaining, smiling man who is constantly alert to see that his customers are satisfied and given every courtesy. He is evidently a keen student of human nature. The other day I overheard him saying to one of his associates, "That customer really liked the way you shined his shoes, Fred. You did a nice job." The other man beamed. It is easy to see why Dr. Shine's men cheerfully cooperate with him to please customers. He appreciates their craving for approval.

WE ALL LIKE TO BE LIKED

"We should not be too selfish in our praise," said Oliver Wendell Holmes, Jr. "People will do more to support a character than to build one."

He meant that when you praise people, they instinctively assume the character you have given them. They actually strive harder to be that character than they would in trying to build up their character voluntarily. Thus, we may say that justifiable approval builds up the character of those we praise.

THE MAKING OF A CHAMPION

The story behind Mr. Holmes' masterly analysis occurred during the Civil War. Holmes was in the Federal Army and was badly in need of a scout. He had in his troop a lanky Virginian named Hatfield who had picked up a good deal of the difficult skill of scouting. One night in the officer's mess, Holmes said to a fellow officer, "You know, Johnson, I think Hatfield is the most capable scout I have ever seen."

This remark soon got around to Corporal Hatfield and it made him a changed man. Where his scouting activities had been good before, they soon became great. He felt he had a reputation to live up to and he made every effort to justify that reputation. He really became a master of it, and all because a wise and just officer had expressed his approval of him.

YOUR APPROVAL MUST BE REAL

One of the ways we can express our approval of our families and associates at the funeral home is by our attitude. In order to put this attitude over, we must really believe that their opinions, selections, surroundings, and background are praiseworthy.

The little pat on the back means everything to approval-starved people. We imply approval when we say such things as: "I like your tie," "Your home is so beautiful," "A person of your experience deserves to be heard," and "You did a nice job today."

But these little expressions of approval must have the ring of sincerity about them. There is no halfway method about it. You must sound like you mean it and look like you mean it, or else you don't get away with it!

HIS KNACK OF APPROVING WINS BUSINESS

A pre-need counselor who sells a tremendous amount of insurance uses this method of approval. Before he even starts to make his presentation, he always looks around the client's home and selects something that he truly thinks is nice and uses that item as a conversational starting place.

For instance, he sees a new chair, a new plant, or a beautiful antique. He compliments the item and the family and then goes into his formal presentation.

CRITICISM MUST BE CONSTRUCTIVE

When you criticize someone's efforts, remember what you so lightly condemn probably represents much conscientious, hopeful toil. It may deserve criticism, but remember the hunger for approval, and let the individual down easy. Compliment the good features first, then constructively point out how better funeral service can be secured. Such criticism is acceptable. When you save the other person's face, you make a friend. Lasting resentment is often created in someone by harsh, contemptuous criticism.

THE DUTY OF A FRIEND

"It is not flattery to give a friend due character," wrote George Washington, "for commendation is the duty of a friend." It is a duty, which, when left undone, denies you the profit to be found in its doing. Considered strictly from your own standpoint as an individual, it is not a question of, "Can you afford to register your approval of others?" The real question for our profession is, "Can you afford not to?"

DISCUSSION QUESTIONS

1. How important is approval for you?

2. When you receive approval, does it inspire you to do better?

3. How do you respond to insincere approval?

4. How do you criticize people?

18

FLATTERY

"Lord, make me humble, but don't let me know it!"

Dwight L. Moody

LEARNING OBJECTIVES

- Explain how flattery merges into insincerity.
- Describe how to handle honest compliments.
- Explain the risk of being insincere.
- Define the term *gentle flattery.*

SOFT-PEDALLING FLATTERY: A LITTLE GOES A LONG WAY

President Calvin Coolidge once told one of his secretaries, "I like honey, but I don't like it spread on too thick." This was just Coolidge's way of saying he liked a little flattery but resented having it piled on.

Most people resent too much flattery, and in the funeral profession the ones who "spread it on too thick" are soon avoided whenever possible.

I once saw a funeral director stand up and introduce a singer at a charity benefit. The funeral director said, "She always makes me think of Natalie Cole. Her voice has charmed millions, and her personality wins everyone she meets. She is smart, beautiful, and talented." He went on and on, and as he piled on a few more layers, the singer turned her back and made faces (indicating nausea) to the other musicians. Then, after singing her two numbers, the singer went over to the funeral director and told him how disgusted she was with his embellishments. She told him straight out that she thought his extremes of flattery were false.

FLATTERY EASILY MERGES INTO INSINCERITY

A little flattery may smooth the way with a family, but in this profession there is a definite line beyond which we must not go. The best way to judge how *not* to overstep the line is to ask ourselves how sincere it *sounds* and *seems*.

As much as he liked applause, Winston Churchill never appreciated insincere, gushing flattery. He was once entertained by a member of Parliament when a woman took him aside and began heaping flattery upon him. Churchill listened, then gently said, "My dear, there may be some impossible fool who corresponds to the remarks you have just made, but thank God it is not Winston Churchill."

HONEST COMPLIMENTS ARE APPRECIATED

Sincere appreciation never goes amiss. Many years ago, the funeral home I worked at handled all the funerals for eight family members who were killed in a tragic fire. My boss did not sleep for three days. After the funerals were over, he sat at his desk with his head in his hands from sheer weariness.

The bookkeeper of the funeral home came into the office and my boss said, "Why, Mary, I thought all the deposits were already made. Are there still more?" "No, sir," said the bookkeeper, "I just came in to tell you how wonderful you were throughout the last couple of days." This was the highest compliment the bookkeeper could think of, and my boss was tremendously touched by her thoughtfulness. You could see his appreciation by how his eyes welled up!

IT IS THE EVIDENCE OF SINCERITY THAT COUNTS

When everyone was praising General Norman Schwarzkopf, he met the Archbishop of Chicago, Joseph Cardinal Bernadin. Cardinal Bernadin grasped Schwarzkopf's hand and simply said, "Great work." That was all, yet it was a statement that the General could sincerely believe, and remember, the excessive flattery was forgotten. Many are hungry for a little appreciation. When people do good work, compliment them. Your genuine appreciation stimulates them to greater effort, and you win their goodwill and cooperation.

WHAT IS UP THE FLATTERER'S SLEEVE?

"Why did you let Bob go?" a friend asked the vice-president of a certain cemetery. (Bob had been head bookkeeper and had climbed to his position over several years). "I'll tell you why," said the vice-president. "According to him, *I* was so marvelous I should have had the president's job. I was so good he usually managed to let me do about a third of his work, so I decided to get someone who thought less of me but did more work."

When someone douses flattery on us, our usual reaction is, "What a line!" Others react just as we do. The desire of the flatterer to "get in with them" backfires, usually to their own disadvantage.

THE ART OF GENTLE FLATTERY

There was a funeral director from Montreal who was a master of the art of gentle flattery. Going through his funeral home one day, his embalmer stopped him to talk. "Mr. Johnson," the embalmer said, "here is a cosmetic combination I have been working on at home in my spare time. What do you think?" The funeral director realized in a flash that the cosmetic concoction was not right, but said, "This looks interesting and I appreciate your effort in working it out. I'll take it up with the embalming fluid representative and report to you later. Meanwhile, I'm glad I have people like you working with me here at the funeral home."

That phrase, "working *with* me" was flattering, but also sincere. He might have said "working for me." That funeral director won a fast friend, and although the cosmetic idea didn't work out, that embalmer eventually developed one which proved highly effective.

USE IT SPARINGLY AND WITH CARE

The right kind of flattery must possess common sense and sincerity. We know that, contrasted with making an honest way in the world and achieving honest success, overdone flattery is just a questionable device by which those of shaky character think extra favors and easy advancement may be gained.

The person who overdoes flattery is mentally dishonest. People like this are not honest with themselves, and they seem to believe that they can get away with it. Use flattery sparingly and with care. It then becomes honest appreciation and is appreciated by families, colleagues, staff, and others.

 DISCUSSION QUESTIONS

1. Describe an experience when you have been flattered so much that you were embarrassed.

2. How do you flatter people?

3. List the pros and cons of flattering and see which comes out first.

4. Describe sincere versus insincere people you have encountered.

III

DIFFICULT
SITUATIONS

"Blessed are the peacemakers: for they shall be called the children of God."

Matthew 5:9

19
CLIENT COMPLAINTS

"All doors are open to courtesy."

Thomas Fuller

LEARNING OBJECTIVES

- Understand the concept that service only begins with a positive relationship.

- Be able to explore the concept of challenges and opportunities.

- Explain the idea that attentiveness must prevail after the service.

- Appreciate the importance of a sympathetic and empathetic attitude.

FUNERAL SERVICE BEGINS AND ENDS WITH SERVICE

The founder of Macy's Department Store in New York once said in a talk to his staff, "I value an expert complaint handler more highly than a person who is only an expert in business. The former will make ten friends to the latter's one."

That may seem an unusual way to look at the complaint problem, but, as we shall see, it is a highly practical attitude.

A successfully handled complaint results first in the grateful friendship of the complainer. Most people who muster the courage to lodge a complaint are usually a little unsure of themselves. The complainer doesn't know how *you* are going to react to the complaint. When people find their complaint handled with consideration and helpfulness, then the complainer

becomes a supporter, and that is precisely the goal of complaint handling.

Many of us, unfortunately, look at complaints as "just more grief." Yet, clients consider it "grief" also, or else they would not make a kick about it.

THE COMPLAINER IS "FOR" OR "AGAINST" YOU

When you turn a client's "grief" into satisfaction, it is only human nature that he should tell his friends about the courteous treatment that has been received at your hands. Complaints that are satisfactorily handled usually result in good news being spread about you, but if satisfaction is withheld, the client will be especially inclined to spread negative news.

A pre-need funeral contract was causing a client a problem. The person could not understand the contract and called the manager of the funeral home that employed the pre-need salesperson who had originally issued the contract.

When the funeral home manager arrived at the client's home, he looked at the contract and then asked the all-important question: "Did Miss Jones explain this to you, ma'am?" "No," was the client's response. Whether Miss Jones did or did not explain the contract was not the immediate issue. The important issue here was that the client was not satisfied.

At once, the manager walked the disturbed client line by line through the document. Then, he said to the client, "Our representative made a serious oversight in not properly explaining each item to you. We certainly owe you an apology, and I'm going to send a written report to Miss Jones regarding it."

The funeral director's sincerity so impressed the client that she replied, "No, don't do that. I'm thinking now that Miss Jones did talk about the contract and I'm probably the stupid one for forgetting. I think I ought to write Miss Jones and apologize for being so forgetful. I've been really upset about this, but now it all seems straight. I guess the laugh is on me!"

A CHALLENGE AND AN OPPORTUNITY

You see the point. Miss Jones probably did explain the contract just fine, but for whatever reason or motivation, the client wanted more attention and more satisfaction. The funeral director handled the complaint very well.

Mr. Leon Spiegel, the late president of the massive mail order house that bore his name, wrote once in his weekly departmental letter: "Every complaint is a challenge and an opportunity—a challenge to our tactfulness and understanding—an opportunity to earn an immediate friend and the friendship of all the complainers."

Spiegel continued, "But don't run away with the idea that we have to give away the house in order to settle complaints satisfactorily. We can't throw in a sofa with every chair. There must be justice in all business matters, and justice involves both the complainers and ourselves. We can and must settle all complaints so judiciously that there will be satisfaction for both sides. Today, we call this the win–win situation."

Every employee of every funeral home, no matter what the position is, is at all times "on the firing line" in the handling of complaints. As funeral professionals, our duty is to see to it that the complaint does *not* turn into a battle. There is a common tendency on the part of most people to first greet the complaining client with coldness. This tendency may be natural, but it indicates a real lack of professional discipline. In other words, many people are courteous enough when money is being transacted, but the subsequent voicing of even a slight complaint makes them clam up and causes the client to feel uncomfortable.

This is particularly dangerous in the funeral profession. When a client complains, we have only one opportunity to create satisfaction, for we cannot repeat a funeral. If we clam up, the consequences can be very unpleasant.

ATTENTION CREATES OBLIGATIONS

When a complaint is made and nothing is done, naturally the client becomes angry. The client has made his or her investment in good faith, believing that it will be satisfactory in every way. Most clients will not understand (and rightfully so) why their complaints are not treated with sympathy and helpfulness instead of iciness and disdain.

A funeral director was handling a military funeral in Wisconsin when she was approached by a family member (a sister-in-law) who said that the flowers on the wreath from the service organization to which the deceased had belonged were wilted and dead.

The funeral director herself had arranged for the wreath. The sister-in-law requested that a new wreath be ordered. The funeral director replied, "There is really nothing wrong with the flowers. If I order another wreath, it will cost more money, and I know you don't want to do that."

The sister-in-law nodded her head and left in silence. The funeral director thought, "Wow, that was a close one!"

Within two hours, the wife of the deceased military person called up and said, "I guess you and I can't get along together on the wreath thing. My sister sobbed for an hour because of the way you treated her. Who do you think you are? We are sending my husband to the XYZ mortuary and we are going to do this today!"

The funeral director broke into a cold sweat. She tried to call to say that a new wreath had been ordered, but the widow refused all calls. Needless to say, the XYZ mortuary arrived within the hour to make the change.

SYMPATHY AND EMPATHY ARE NOT DEAD— THEY ARE IMPORTANT!

As funeral professionals, we pride ourselves on our ability to be sympathetic and empathetic. We should always listen to complaints with the sincere sympathy that we use when a bereaved family is pouring their heart out to us. The more understanding and helpful we are, the more quickly we will "smooth down the ruffled feather."

I once worked for a funeral director who had made an art out of the ability to smooth down the ruffled feather. When a client would make a complaint, this funeral director actually went overboard by intention. In other words, he seemed more affronted at what was unsatisfactory than did the client. He would direct orders, he would be ashamed, and, in fact, he would make such a fuss that the clients would begin to feel a little ashamed of their complaint and would ask him to forget it. "No, no, no. This cannot happen here. I will not stand for it." This funeral director flooded his complaining clients with strong attention. Eventually, the client would smile, the funeral director would smile, and everything moved along smoothly.

Today, these exaggerations may seem slightly funny to us, but they serve as a magnified and exaggerated example of how properly handled complaints turn the complainer into a satisfied client.

THE GOLDEN RULE OF BUSINESS: DEAL AS YOU WOULD BE DEALT WITH

In helping others in your funeral home, the issue of complaints is inevitable, and the skillful complaint handler has an outstandingly important role to fill.

Handling complaints demands study and practice, and *you alone*, as a funeral service practitioner, can develop and even perfect this ability for yourself. It is more than worth all the effort you give it, for it will strengthen you in every funeral experience and will gain you an enviable professional skill.

 DISCUSSION QUESTIONS

1. Why is it important to satisfy every complaint?

2. Describe an expert complaint handler.

3. How should we look at a complaint?

4. What can happen if you mishandle a complaint?

20

THE CYNIC

"Do the best you can. That's bad enough."

Anthony C. Lund

LEARNING OBJECTIVES

- Explain how a sympathetic viewpoint softens the cynical attitude.

- Explain how tactful modesty is the safest way to communicate with a cynic.

- Understand how difficult it can be to win a cynic's confidence.

- Explain and give examples of what sincere service is all about.

THE PROBLEM OF WINNING CONFIDENCE

As all funeral professionals know, the cynical family is difficult to deal with because they are suspicious and they discount much of what you say. This is always an uneasy situation.

Somewhere in their experience, the cynics have been disillusioned. They usually question everything they are told, and their doubts are not easily satisfied. Families with this make-up usually think they have the straight story and see themselves as experts, and in today's world, many of them really know a good deal about what we have to offer.

A wise man once said that, "A cynic is a fellow who knows all about it, but is willing to learn more if you know how to teach him."

SYMPATHETIC VIEWPOINT SOFTENS THE CYNIC

It is a good strategy, and it truly works—for a funeral professional to be impressed by the cynical client's apparent knowledge. Present your facts with sincerity and with quiet confidence, without forcing your views. Assume that you know that clients "cannot be fooled," that you respect their judgment, and that you are merely submitting information upon which they will make their own decisions. Do not get in an ego match. Your sincere, helpful attitude will gradually dispel their skepticism and cynicism and capture their confidence. There is really not a safe alternative in dealing with a cynic, for if you prove yourself correct and them wrong, the damage created is simply not worth it.

The president of a large department store was quite a flower fancier who was proud of his garden. He went to a nursery for some tulip bulbs and talked like an expert to the nurseryman. He began to order bulbs, flipping off the names like a veteran. The nurseryman, a native of Holland, realized that this man was a cynic and really did not know that much about tulip bulbs. The nurseryman made a few suggestions concerning new species that he felt might be added to the wide selection being made. His suggestions, however, were rejected.

Finally, the nurseryman said, "You are quite an expert on tulips, Mr. Brandies, and have made some very interesting selections. However, I do not think all of them are quite worthy of your gardens. A number of the varieties you have listed are out of date, while I know you are fundamentally as much interested in the newer species as the gardener who created them in Holland. Some of these are so new here you could not possibly have heard of them, for they have just arrived." The cynical client was impressed and left the whole matter of the selection up to the veteran nurseryman.

MODEST, TACTFUL ATTITUDE USUALLY DISPELS CYNICISM AND SKEPTICISM

This clever nurseryman played right along with the cynical man and turned an ordinary sale of cheap bulbs into a substantial order for high-priced, fancy stock.

When we contact a suspicious, doubting mind, an immediate danger to us is that the cynic's attitude may influence our negativity! If this happens, the cynic has won a victory over the

funeral professional. However, we do have a wall of defense
that the cynic cannot penetrate—our absolute sincerity of purpose. That which we do in our funeral homes is of inestimable
worth. Cynics may mentally, even verbally, try to laugh off the
sincere and honest attitude of quality service, but all the time
they are being impressed by it!

A FUNERAL DIRECTOR OVERCOMES A CYNIC

A man sat in the arrangement conference room with his
daughter and the funeral director. The man glared at the funeral director and said, "We know what you people do. I've
read *The American Way of Death!*" The funeral director smiled
and said, "Oh, yes, I read that book many years ago. It was very
interesting. What impressed you most about it?" The man was
dumbfounded. "Well, I, oh, well." The funeral director then
said, "The book made a significant impact, and while it did expose some problems, it really changed this great profession for
the better." "How so?" inquired the man. "Well, it helped
tighten up regulatory boards; it inspired us to teach new
courses in our mortuary training, like "psychology of grief";
and it helped us to look more critically at ourselves. While it exaggerated a lot, all in all, it was positive." "I didn't realize all
that!" the man replied.

This funeral director had diffused the cynic by taking the
high road. He did not react—he taught. He did not fold up—
he told the truth. The man later admitted that he had really
never read *The American Way of Death,* but his minister had advised him to say that to put the funeral director on the defensive. It didn't work!

THE SINCERE DESIRE TO SERVE MAKES A WIN–WIN

You get the point. It was the sincere desire and interest of the
funeral director and his expert knowledge about *The American
Way of Death,* and funeral service in general, that turned the
cynic into an ally and paved the way for a valuable service experience. This funeral director was armored against that cynical
attitude, and he won a skillful victory over it.

In the case of cynical and skeptical minds, you must meet
their criticism, put-downs, and wisecracks with the quiet confidence in your own mind that the funeral service you offer is
definitely right, that your knowledge of it is complete, and that

you are the reliable kind of person whose sincere and helpful attitude cannot be turned aside by the cynical, skeptical pose.

And most of it is a pose. When you get under the surface of a cynical person, you usually find a warm-hearted, flesh-and-blood human being. Maybe this person has been taken advantage of or mistreated occasionally and can't forget. These are things to keep in mind as you contact a cynic.

Never forget that all their ratty acidity can be neutralized and made harmless by your ability to remain sincere, honest, and helpful.

 ## DISCUSSION QUESTIONS

1. Describe the cynical client—what is he or she often like underneath?

2. What are several strategies for dealing with the cynic?

3. How can you spot the cynic?

4. Discuss a situation where you handled a cynical client successfully.

21

COOLNESS UNDER FIRE

A Trait Greatly Admired By Others

"What a day may bring a day may take away."
Thomas Fuller

 LEARNING OBJECTIVES

- Explain how self-control develops character.

- Understand the importance of attitude when being criticized.

- Describe how different characters in the same funeral home can rise or fall by how they handle pressure.

- Explain why keeping the voice down is so important.

Funeral professionals who fly off the handle at the first sign of confusion or conflict arouse contempt and antagonism. It is natural to admire the person who is calm, poised, and resourceful when things go wrong—and things do go wrong at funerals!

How many of us are prepared to keep every situation well in hand by the very force of our own calmness, by our absolute refusal to be flustered no matter what comes up? When we cultivate "coolness under fire," we will have a powerful advantage in dealing with others.

SELF-CONTROL DEVELOPS CHARACTER

Every day in your work at the funeral home or in social relations, some disturbance or disagreement is apt to develop un-

expectedly. The hearse driver has not worn a white shirt, the family is late for the service, or the bouquet of flowers looks terrible. As all funeral directors know, on those days your good nature and self-control will be put to the test. Your ability to think and act clearly may save a friend or a family or preserve harmony throughout the entire funeral home.

A few years ago, a funeral procession was on the way to the cemetery to bury an archbishop. Halfway to the cemetery, the hearse blew a radiator hose. The funeral director calmly pulled over, reached behind the seat, got a roll of duct tape, wrapped the break in the hose, and proceeded to the cemetery.

A funeral professional with self-control and a cool head is always bigger by comparison than one lacking such qualities. Think of the insight that funeral director had to have to put a roll of duct tape in the funeral coach just for such an emergency! Families are inspired with that type of coolness, and they believe that such a person is worthy of confidence.

THE BADGE OF CHARACTER

Woodrow Wilson, when he was President of the United States, wrote to a friend, "I believe the greatest victories in war, in business, and personal success are achieved by maintaining coolness and singleness of purpose under fire. In times of great stress and strain, true ability and worth stand out more dramatically than under softer conditions."

BE BIGGER THAN YOUR CRITIC

The funeral profession, over the last three decades, has been a target of some rough criticisms by the media. While we all know that most of the huff is exaggerated, it still stings. The worst thing a funeral director can do is to panic or fly off the handle when such trials are directed his way.

We are all acquainted with that famous painting of "Whistler's Mother." There she sits serenely, as one who has met all of life's battles with coolness and great courage. By contrast, her son, James MacNeil Whistler, went through life in a constant state of fury at his critics, his friends, and everyone else. When the critics derided his art, he couldn't take it. Had he coolly and constructively explained his technique, the world might sooner have appreciated his greatness. He never lived to hear himself acclaimed as the genius he was, and died embittered.

When you are dealing with an angry, accusing person, let him talk himself out. Keep cool, and aim to serve that person and adjust the trouble fairly. Your attitude will often win that person over.

RISE OF A TROUBLESHOOTER

A funeral apprentice was sent to straighten out the complaint of a family who thought the register book had been poorly completed. When the young apprentice arrived at the residence, he was met with a barrage of profanity and excited claims that turned the air blue. However young he was, instead of yielding to the temptation to make heated replies, he remained calm and said nothing, while the family ranted and raved. Finally, having had their say, the family turned to the apprentice and one of them said, "You're all right, son. We feel better just getting this thing out. Can you fix this mess?"

This was the trouble-shooting apprentice's cue, and indicating a sympathetic understanding, he quickly showed the family how the trouble could be overcome. Thus, he made powerful friends for himself and the funeral home.

A STUDY IN CONTRAST

It is interesting to watch two employees as they grow up in a funeral business. One seems "on the upgrade," almost from the start. The other gets ahead very slowly. Is it luck? It is far more than that.

Many years ago, two young men joined a funeral home in Chicago. The owner had no children. Both men were about the same age, height, and general appearance. Both were fully licensed. Within nineteen years, "A" became president of the funeral home. The other fellow, "F," despite many different jobs in the funeral home, never got to be more than a staff person.

Disposition certainly had something to do with the difference in their fortunes. "A" could not be flustered. He was calm and patient, sincerely interested in the families' problems and difficulties. No matter how hostile a family might be over some real or fancied slight, they had but to talk to "A" a few minutes to go away feeling satisfied.

"F" was a combination of grouch and volcano. From the beginning, if a family complained about the service, "F" prided himself on his ability to "dodge those weirdos!" How he managed to hold his job was a mystery.

Self-control under fire is the ironbound element of character to cultivate if we want to be in control of every situation in the funeral home no matter how vexing.

COOL-HEADEDNESS CALMS FAMILIES

In the funeral profession, it is wise and safe to figure that families we service will mostly be somewhat nervous and keyed up. It is the nature of dealing with death and grief. Most bereaved families have never practiced self-control; most people seem to never think they have to. It is precisely for this reason that they react to your calmness and coolness in a positive way.

KEEP THE VOICE DOWN

One of the great skills under fire is to keep the voice down. Let the family or the other person do the loud talking. Your quietness shows them up, and they quickly realize this. When you handle them this way, they will calm down in short order and fairly eat out of your hand.

Few people have a natural ability to be cool under fire. Most of us, therefore, have to develop the trait. It is not as difficult as it might seem. The largest part of the secret is in refusing to be moved by difficult situations. The rest of it is self-control.

When you incur someone's anger, and we all do, this philosophical attitude is a help: "This person has not learned the advantage of self-control. He is showing his weakness by being loud and abusive. I show my power by being calm and patient."

Never forget that this one element of character can make a funeral director a power in any group, be it in his family, with employees, or with social or business contacts.

 DISCUSSION QUESTIONS

1. How can we cultivate coolness under fire?

2. Is there any way to foresee and prevent a vexing situation?

3. What happens if a situation continues to grow out of control?

4. Think of an instance in which you exercised coolness. Share with the group what happened.

22

HANDLING THE
DIFFICULT FAMILY

"Adversity has ever been considered the state in which a man most easily becomes acquainted with himself."

Samuel Johnson

 LEARNING OBJECTIVES

- Explain why it is important to let people express their frustrations.
- Understand why some people enjoy being difficult.
- Know how to exert self-control in these situations.
- Explain how to turn frustration into satisfaction.

The Chinese say that when a person is arguing heatedly with someone and begins to fight, that person has run out of ideas. That is a good thing to remember when dealing with a grouchy family or person. You may feel like arguing, but you can control the situation with ideas and win the family for a friend.

LET THEM "BLOW OFF STEAM"

A difficult or grouchy family either has something on their mind that makes them angry or they feel bad physically. Given what we know about grief—well, in our profession, the odds are high that people may not feel all that great and have highly pressing issues on their minds!

Families may look fierce, bark their questions and orders, and even make sarcastic and unkind remarks. Whatever the cause, permit the venting to spend itself.

Families usually cannot continue to be angry with you when your every effort shows that you have their interests at heart and truly want to serve them. As a funeral professional, you do not want to fight, because *you* have not run out of ideas. Patiently, try to gain their point of view and always feel kindly toward them. Such an attitude possesses magic properties.

Families handled this way usually calm down and become human again, but they also can begin to feel secretly ashamed. Often, to make amends for their treatment of you, they will become an even more generous and complimentary person or group.

DON'T SPOIL THEIR FUN

As problematic as this idea can be, it is nonetheless true—some families and people simply enjoy being ill-tempered. So, as funeral professionals, our job in this case is to be polite and considerate and show the gloomy people that you have their welfare at heart. Don't spoil their fun. Just as other people enjoy ill health, some enjoy their ill temper. They might respond to sympathy, genuine interest, and good service. You can be guaranteed that they will respond to distant or ill-tempered attitudes from the funeral professional, and the response will not be pleasant. Our only alternative is to risk being genuine and sympathetic and give them great service.

ONLY A TV GROUCH CAN GET AWAY WITH IT

Don Rickles, the famous grouch character actor, is said to be a very pleasant person in real life. In his acting, he gets paid to put on a long face and voice harsh, disparaging remarks. Yet, he is the first to admit that such a temperament would be a big handicap in actual life.

We can laugh at Rickles on television, but it's no joke for anyone to parade his or her grouchy side in the presence of families and funeral home associates. Nor is it funny when we lose friends and families because we forget to smile and, instead, give an exhibition of impatience and ill temper. Molasses, as Abraham Lincoln said, draws more flies than vinegar—a good thing to remember in dealing with a grouch or curbing the grouch in ourselves.

KEEP COOL

The easiest thing one can do is to reflect a grouch's mood and snap him back. That is a sign of weakness and cannot win the patronage or goodwill of such a client. Quiet enjoyment can be gained by working on a grouchy client with diplomacy and goodwill, and watching him soften under your friendliness and spirit of service.

A chauffeur in a funeral home once remarked how grouchy and touchy some families are. It is to be expected because they are grieving. Some families curse him, some ignore him, and some are downright nasty to him. Several times, he himself had just cause for righteous indignation due to the grouchiness of the families he transported, but through it all, he drove unconcerned about the abuse.

The chauffeur's formula was simple: He knew the families' stress and problems were greater than his, so he would never get excited. He would do all he could for them and then would just keep cool.

NOT A BAD SORT WHEN YOU KNOW THEM

The grouch or grouchy families are not as bad as they seem. They don't have horns and a forked tail all the time. At other times and in other circumstances, they are undoubtedly charming. All the rough talk and glowering looks may be simply a way of covering up. When you refuse to let them get you down and you maintain your poise, they will respect you. Then, you, as a professional, have won a client and a friend.

 DISCUSSION QUESTIONS

1. Are you familiar with the family that needs to blow off steam?

2. Why is it even more important to be pleasant and give good service to a client who is ill-tempered or gloomy?

3. How can we curb the grouch in ourselves?

4. Have you ever discovered that the grouch really is not so bad underneath?

23

GETTING BACK IN THEIR GOOD GRACES

"The greatest sin against mankind is not to hate them—but to be indifferent to them."
George Bernard Shaw

 LEARNING OBJECTIVES

- Explain how to find and quickly remove the cause of resentment.

- Understand how customers are sensitive.

- Explain and know how to make amends quickly.

- Appreciate the importance of customer pride.

FIND AND QUICKLY REMOVE THE CAUSE OF RESENTMENT

We all have had the sad experience of unexpectedly losing the goodwill of a family. Often, we see no reason whatsoever for the break in the former cordial relationship the family had with the funeral home. If the truth be known, we also realize that many times thoughtless words or actions on our part might have been the cause.

All our lives, we are constantly engaged in a "conflict of personalities." The other person's interests usually comes first, and our diplomacy as funeral professionals in dealing with others should always start from that point.

When we study our own makeup and realize how sensitive most of us are underneath the brusque exterior, we can understand our fellow human beings feel the same way.

Pride is often seen as a negative thing, but in reality, pride is a tremendously important factor in human relationships. When we show neglect, indifference, or contempt, the other person suffers a blow to his or her pride, and that is when trouble usually starts. Soothing the other person's pride is one way back into his or her goodwill.

FAMILIES ARE SENSITIVE

A hard lesson in funeral service is that it is often what we do *not* do, rather than what we do, that causes broken relationships with families.

A certain funeral home in a Midwest community had for years placed a door badge on the front door of the building to signify a death. The community grew very accustomed to this symbol because there was only a weekly newspaper, and the door badge was a method to send word of the death of someone.

Eventually, the funeral home was sold to a young man who was unfamiliar with the door badge symbol and who, furthermore, thought the custom was old-fashioned. The next death he had, the young funeral director did *not* put out the funeral door badge. He overlooked a "rite" and soon he learned that his community was peeved. Now, you may think the community showed a rather small side of their nature, but the public is often that way. Little things upset them and their pride, and these people were proud of their door badges!

The young funeral director should have displayed the door badge, and over the next several services he conducted, he moved heaven and earth to right the neglect and win the public back. He acted quickly but ate considerable "humble pie."

AMENDS MUST BE MADE QUICKLY

A tremendously important point in getting back in a family's good graces is the quick follow-up. An unintentional slight word, for whatever reason rubbed the wrong way, grows and rankles and becomes more bitter with every hour and every day it is not explained.

A highly successful funeral director who had won success without ever using an advertising agency finally decided to appoint one. The news spread quickly. First to call was the representative of a well-known agency. He told the funeral director of the fine results his organization had produced for other companies and outlined its complete facility for handling the funeral home's account. He was working a favorable impression on the funeral director until suddenly he made a fatal mistake. The funeral director stated that the final advertising contract would be made on a competitive basis. Instead of tactfully agreeing that such a conclusion was logical and leaving it on its own merit, the salesman bluntly pooh-poohed the idea.

HE HURT THE FUNERAL DIRECTOR'S PRIDE

The funeral director's attitude suddenly cooled, and he called the conference to a quick close. The salesman knew his product thoroughly but knew little about the workings of human nature. He needed to learn that you cannot scoff at the ideas of others, no matter how ridiculous they may seem, and still retain their goodwill.

THE SPIRIT THAT WINS THEM BACK

As funeral professionals, when we sincerely try to recapture the goodwill of some customer or friend, that individual often responds in the same spirit. Much depends on the desire in your heart to make amends if the fault is yours, or to find the cause of dissatisfaction in order to make things right.

There is not a funeral director alive who has not suffered through the anxiety of seeing a family once served go to another funeral home. Most often, these suffering funeral directors do their suffering in silence, but silence solves nothing.

What works is to gently inquire after the funeral is completed as to what services were unsatisfactory, or what may have been misunderstood in the last service. It shows honest concern for your families to express a charitable attitude of attention toward a family even after they patronized your competitor without telling you why.

By gently confronting this situation, you will also learn a great deal about how people really feel about your operation.

By showing attention to a lost family, you will indicate your desire to serve them even after their patronage was apparently lost. It just may be that your call will soften them and help re-gain them next time to engage your services.

HUMBLE PIE WON'T HURT YOU

It is a fact that eating humble pie is often the only way we can re-establish ourselves in the good graces of our families. As the late Vice-President Thomas Marshall once said, "Humble pie isn't bad eating when you know that there will be a restored friendship for dessert."

Of course, the best human relations system is to be ever watchful in preserving goodwill. There will be no wounds to heal and no explanation necessary. To be an expert in the right thing to say and the right thing to do at the right time, and never to cause resentment by negligence or inattention, are priceless ingredients in the formula for funeral professionals to successfully deal with others.

 DISCUSSION QUESTIONS

1. How can you identify the cause of family resentment?

2. How can you remove the cause?

3. Why are families so sensitive?

4. How can you be more humble?

24

THE UNREASONABLE FAMILY

"My life is in the hands of any fool who makes me lose my temper."

Dr. John Hunter

 LEARNING OBJECTIVES

- Understand the concept of giving people their money's worth.

- Know how to see the family's point of view.

- Explain how to give service that is remembered.

- Explain the dangers of being impatient with a family.

WE MERELY WANT OUR MONEY'S WORTH

There is an old story in the Midwest about the proud mother who went to see her son, Jim, march in a drill team and later proudly remarked, "Yes, it was wonderful, but do you know they were all out of step but Jim."

This applies to the funeral professional who gets the idea that the family is unreasonable—that they are all out of step but him.

Families, even ones in the midst of grief, are no more unreasonable than any other individuals. Finances are naturally a concern for them, no more or less than when you or I step out to spend our money. As most in this profession already know, when a family invests their money, they want service with a capital "S."

When we are buying, each of us is self-centered in our desire to be completely satisfied. Many want the expectation of service to be exceeded! It seems to be human nature, and that is not unreasonable.

SEE THE FAMILY'S VIEWPOINT

A funeral director in Phoenix, Arizona, once had a family that was changing their minds constantly concerning the color schemes and hardware on caskets. Later, an apprentice asked the funeral director if he was exasperated by the way some families constantly changed their minds. "No," said the funeral director, "that family has to live with the decisions they make, so why shouldn't they be particular? Anyway, I really like the fussy family better than the one too easy to suit. The fussy family is making absolutely sure that everything is to their taste. The other type of family doesn't let you know what they don't like, and that can be dangerous." That is the kind of service philosophy that every funeral and cemetery professional should hold.

SERVICE THAT STICKS

A famous New York City funeral director tells his colleagues that the number one mission is to satisfy and exceed the expectations of their families. He wants his funeral director to discuss every aspect of their services. Go to every extent, no matter how unreasonable, to prove to the family that your price is sound and justifiable. That kind of service sticks; it makes the family content and boosts the funeral home.

Some of us are inclined to get our backs up at the seeming ill nature and impatience on the part of families. That is wrong because the family really hasn't "got it in for us" at all. Families are often thoughtless, and with many today it is simply the old case of "pocketbook manners." They are spending the money, and they think that *we* are the ones who should watch our manners, *not themselves!* Sad, but true—they are right.

CASKET REP COULD TAKE IT

A highly successful casket representative is remembered mostly for the high-quality caskets he sold. He was a master salesman. He kept a corner on the lion's share of the casket business and was once asked to what he attributed his continuous success. He responded, "When there's a big deal in the making, these owners can be meaner than a pack of wolves. They demand the best deal. I just step right in the middle of them and let them tear me to pieces like a lamb. When the fur quits flying, I walk out with the order."

The casket rep's message was that it did not make any difference to him how unreasonable the customer seemed, as long he got the business.

ARE YOU ALWAYS REASONABLE?

I worked for a funeral director years ago who had the following situation happen. One of the other directors stormed into his office and shouted, "I want you to fire Mary. She made a big mistake yesterday and she tried to lie her way out of it." My boss replied, "Did her mistake hurt the family and did it cost us a lot of money?" The answer to both questions was, "No." Then, my boss asked the agitated man, "Did you ever make a mistake? Did you ever tell a lie?"

The moral of this story is never try to pluck the splinter from another's eye while there is a beam in your own.

IMPATIENCE DRIVES FAMILIES AWAY

A pre-need funeral counselor had a funeral contract almost completed. The funeral was a low-cost service with a cremation container. Out of the blue, the husband asked, "Are any limousines standard with this service?" The pre-need counselor replied, "Sir, you can't expect those extras on a low-priced funeral like this."

The husband froze. "I only wanted to know so I could make arrangements later for one if it was not included. I was just asking." The pre-need counselor was immediately all smiles, but it was too late. The husband cancelled the contract. The safe attitude is that the public is never unreasonable, even when they may be.

FAMILIES APPRECIATE UNSELFISH SERVICE

As professionals in the remembrance and memorialization profession, we should remember that each family we serve is always thinking about themselves—first, last, and always. When we render unselfish service, it is appreciated. This brings swift and positive response, even from the rude and unthinking families.

We must table our egos, lighten up our own self-importance, and realize that the buying public is really a mighty fine bunch of people with money to spend, which will ensure our success and that of our great funeral homes.

DISCUSSION QUESTIONS

1. Discuss how you expect to get your money's worth when you buy something.

2. Is this concept applicable to funeral service?

3. To what extent would you go in service to a family?

4. Are you a patient person, and are you prepared to offer unselfish service?

25

THE SILENT FAMILY

"A soft answer turneth away wrath; but grievous words
stir up anger."
Proverbs 15:1

 LEARNING OBJECTIVES

- Be able to communicate with the silent family.

- Appreciate how silence often denotes a cautious nature.

- Explain how silence is sometimes a defensive front.

- Understand how action can be better than words.

PRY OPEN TIGHT LIPS WITH THE RIGHT QUESTIONS

We are all familiar with the sphinx. She just sits there staring off into space. The sphinxes we meet in the funeral home are truly riddles. It is our task as funeral directors to help solve the human riddle by bringing them out of their silence through skillful handling.

There are many varieties of the silent family. Truth is, most "sphinx" families are silent because they are not quite sure what to do, or sure of what they want. They are not intentionally being difficult. They are simply in a difficult position.

A CASE FOR ACTION—NOT WORDS

It took no imagination on the funeral director's part to see that this man was in no mood to talk. Seeking a little more information, the funeral director asked, "Have you thought about what services you would like for your wife?" The answer came back swiftly and harshly: "Cremation." Analyzing the man's response, the funeral director decided this was a case for action, not a lot of words, and proceeded to map out every conceivable option, and show this man every possible item of merchandise for a cremation service. The funeral director did things for the man instead of talking him to death.

In the end, the man purchased a sizeable service which originally started out with just one word—"cremation."

SILENCE OFTEN DENOTES A CAUTIOUS NATURE

Some families are just silent by nature. They have probably been imposed upon a number of times, and their bump of caution is so big they refuse to open up until you have told them that you and your funeral home are truly there to help them through a tremendous crisis period.

I served a family once who absolutely would not talk. I would ask a question about vital statistics and they just sat there silently. Finally, one of the daughters began to weep and confessed that the family had a terror of funeral homes and had never been in one before this experience.

The arrangement conference came to an abrupt halt and I gave them a tour, got them coffee and Danish, showed them every room in the building, and generally tried to make them comfortable. An hour later, the arrangement conference started again and there was a world of difference.

In less than an hour, we were finished. I believe had I plowed on, without the consideration of a break, I would have driven that family into further silence and distance. I probably would have just antagonized them by talking too much, by assuming just what I wanted to accomplish, and by assuming a familiarity before the ice really broke.

SILENCE IS OCCASIONALLY "PUT ON"

Some of these silent ones take this position toward funeral directors simply as a pose. They actually get a kick out of it. I once had a family in the selection room and they had narrowed their choice to three caskets. Without boosting any one of the caskets, I explained fully the differences and advantages of each. The family just stood there, not uttering a word.

Finally, the son looked at me and said, "Do it again." So I started all over again. I went through the same process and had just started to review the merits of the third casket when the son started grinning at me. "That's all right," he said, "I just wanted to see if you could tell the same story twice." He had his fun and was ready to get down to business.

The silent family is often silent in order to get all the facts without disclosing their weak points (e.g., fear, grief, economics). To get under their veneer, and to see what progress you are making, ask them open-ended questions: "What has been your experience with this?" or "What do you think?"

Few silent families can withstand the challenge of an open-ended question. Once the family warms up and talks, they are no longer the sphinx, and your principal problem in serving them has been solved.

 DISCUSSION QUESTIONS

1. Expand the list of questions you could ask a silent family.

2. Offer examples of how your actions can be more helpful than your words.

3. Discuss situations in which you are silent.

4. How would you handle the silent family? Make a list of ideas.

IV

FUNERAL
DIRECTOR SKILLS

"Perhaps any of us could get along with perfect people.
But our task is to get along with imperfect people."

Richard L. Evans

26

CONFIDENTIALITY

The Essential Ingredient for a Funeral Service Professional

> *"Self trust is the essence of heroism."*
> *Ralph Waldo Emerson*

LEARNING OBJECTIVES

- Understand that confidentiality is the essential ingredient for a funeral director.

- Explain how forgetting a secret is the best way to keep a secret.

- Understand the relationships between keeping a secret and keeping a family.

- Incorporate the skill of insult before the dishonor of breaking a confidence.

"Listen, can you keep a secret? I heard . . ." or "She told me not to say a word about it, but listen . . ." Phrases such as these represent professional suicide for any funeral service practitioner.

In the funeral service profession, confidentialities translate into one single word—trust. Betraying confidences is not just dangerous in the funeral service profession, it can be catastrophic. It is "mental dishonesty." The funeral director who listens to confidences and then makes them public is sowing a whirlwind of ill will.

WHAT YOU DON'T SAY CAN'T COME BACK TO YOU

Calvin Coolidge, a master in confidentiality, once remarked that, "If you never say anything, you will never be asked to repeat it." While this sentiment may be overstated when it comes to professional confidences, Coolidge was right on the mark.

A prominent New York businessman died some years ago. The family selected a reputable funeral director to handle the service. It so happened that in the course of taking the vital statistics, a member of the family confessed that many years ago the deceased had fathered a son out of wedlock. It was always a closely guarded family secret, and while the man took care of his son financially, the family wanted no mention of the incident. It was confidential.

After the family left the arrangement conference, the funeral director went to the staff lounge for a refreshment. The funeral director sat talking to one of the gardeners and eventually leaned over and said, "Listen, can you keep a secret?" "Of course I can," replied the gardener.

It took three months for the family to discover that what they had requested to be kept confidential became public. The family was outraged and rightly so.

The funeral director was terrified that his reputation would be ruined and subsequently criticized the gardener for his breach of conduct. In reality, the fault was not with the gardener. The fault lay entirely in the lap of the funeral director.

When a client confides in a funeral director, it is due to a common human trait—the desire to talk the matter out with someone. As professionals, funeral directors should feel flattered to be chosen as the recipients of family and personal confidence. We should lend such advice or encouragement as we are able, and then forget the whole thing. Forget the secrets. Forgetting the secret is absolutely the best way to keep a secret. When we keep confidences this way, it is surprising how quickly one can gain the reputation for being close-mouthed, a person to whom others can talk safely. This ability is known as *trust*.

LISTEN, CARE, ATTEND, AND FORGET IT!

Oliver Wendell Holmes, Jr., the famous Associate Justice of the United States Supreme Court, once remarked, "A wise man's ear has no bottom. For when someone pours into it his confidences, they vanish and never again come to the surface."

Respecting the confidences of clients and also fellow work associates at the funeral home is an absolute necessity. "Bean spillers" can and do raise a tumult even in the smoothest-running facility.

KEEP A SECRET—KEEP YOUR CLIENTS

Not long ago, a funeral director in San Francisco had a suicide case. The family requested that no one be told of the mode of death. The funeral director gave his word that the secret would be kept.

Not many people came to the visitation period, but about 8:00 P.M., an elderly couple entered, signed the register, and were escorted to the chapel by the funeral director. In the course of their conversation, the elderly man expressed surprise at the sudden death and inquired as to the cause. The funeral director looked around and said, "The family told me not to say a word about it, but . . ."

The elderly couple said nothing and left. One hour later, the daughter of the deceased man called and instructed the funeral director to take her father's remains to the funeral home down the street.

The elderly man was a great uncle. He and his wife were the very people that the family wanted shielded from the knowledge of the suicide. Worse yet, the old gentleman was a retired District Court judge who had legions of influential and prominent friends.

This funeral director slipped badly. He lost not only the immediate funeral service of the suicide victim, but also untold potential opportunities for serving other families in his community.

INSULT BEFORE DISHONOR

Consider the case of a Chicago funeral director who suffered the insults of the news media rather than betray the confidence of a family who had asked him to keep confidential the cause of death of their father. The media called this funeral director repeatedly for the cause of death. The deceased was a person who had a national reputation. Regardless of the pressure to get his name in the paper, this funeral director held his ground. The newspaper reporters grew very insistent, but nothing could sway the funeral director. He had effectively forgotten the family secret. His "forgetfulness" frustrated the media but endeared him to the family.

WATCH WHAT YOU SAY

When you guard your word with your clients, they realize very quickly that you are a trustworthy person. Because you do not spread the confidences of others, they feel they can confide in you with safety. Doctors, lawyers, clergy, and funeral directors deal with some of the most sensitive and confidential situations in a community. They could never survive if they betrayed the countless confidences they hear.

THE VETERAN FUNERAL DIRECTOR

A veteran funeral director, who was literally famous in his community for being in everything, seen everywhere, and knowing everyone, once said, "I have never, ever, violated a confidence—nor would I. That would be, for me, professional suicide."

Trust and confidentiality are vital attributes of the funeral profession. Keep faith with your client by always forgetting their secrets.

 DISCUSSION QUESTIONS

1. Why is confidentiality so essential?

2. How can we resist telling a secret?

3. Is there a special way to handle the media?

4. What will tell us that we are doing a good job?

27

THE POWER OF NAMES

"Who hath not owned, with rapture-smitten frame, the power of grace, the magic of a name."

William Cowper

 LEARNING OBJECTIVES

- Be able to explain why names are so important.
- Understand how familiarity breeds resentment.
- Explain the process for remembering names.
- Understand how getting a name wrong gets you in wrong.

THE IMPORTANCE OF NAMES

A person's name and what it represents to that person is extremely significant. It may not be as glamorous as Robert Redford or carry the influence of the name of the President of the United States, but a person's name means everything to that person. It is the label on the package that contains a personality. A name is the world's means of identifying a living, breathing self.

Everyone regards his or her name as important. It is human nature, and everyone dislikes having their name miscalled. It puts a person in a class with the numberless herd—a nobody.

In funeral service, you are in contact with the public constantly, and you can bring clients and goodwill to your funeral home by getting the names straight. It will help to avoid costly errors and be an important factor in your progress. Likewise, treating the names of fellow associates considerately will aid harmony and efficiency.

An often overlooked cause of ill will is the use of nicknames or contractions of names. Certain individuals thoughtlessly or maliciously kid some other person about his or her name, or pin some silly name on the person that starts others in the habit of doing so. The victims may not always show annoyance, but often a secret resentment burns hotly and finds outlets in many strange ways.

FAMILIARITY BREEDS RESENTMENT

Only very close friends can use our names lightly, and even they must not go too far. You, as a funeral associate, will greatly help to promote harmony among your associates and business acquaintances by treating their names respectfully. Fred Smith may object to being called "Smitty," or even "Smith," by casual acquaintances. He will always appreciate being called "Mr. Smith" at first.

Bringing this concept of familiarity close to home, it is the rare funeral professional who encourages and actually enjoys being called "Digger." All people have much personal dignity, and we all expect a standard of respect when we interact with each other.

Familiarity breeds contempt, and you will always protect yourself by treating the other person *and their name* with dignity and respect at all times.

If the person you are contacting at the moment has a foreign name, difficult to spell or pronounce, be even more alert to getting it right. It will be a feather in your cap.

People with complicated names will no doubt have had trouble with the name elsewhere, and if *you* spell and pronounce it correctly, you will win that person's confidence where others fail. The issue is so sensitive that many people, particularly people with names that are difficult to spell or pronounce, or unusual names that have provided amusement, have gone to the trouble to have their names legally changed. Is it wise to treat lightly, or incorrectly, a name that means so much to its owner?

GETTING NAMES WRONG GETS YOU IN WRONG

Suppose a funeral home, paying thousands of dollars to have its name advertised through a huge electric sign, were to discover the firm's name had been misspelled on the sign. What a roar of complaining would go up! Individuals have that same reaction when their names are misspelled or mispronounced.

Getting a client's name wrong or using it disrespectfully may result in serious disadvantage to you and your funeral home. Here is how the head of a funeral home got in trouble by getting a client's name wrong: A man had made an appointment to talk with this funeral director concerning a pre-arrangement. The man arrived at the funeral home and was asked to wait a few minutes until the funeral director returned from conducting a service. The man sat outside the arrangement office, which was located about fifteen feet from the door of the funeral director's office. The funeral director returned and the prearrangement client heard him say, "Who is this man Voight you say is waiting for me?" Now, that was close to the sound of the man's name, but it was *not* his name.

When the secretary of the funeral home came back, the client was gone. The man later phoned to complain and to let the firm know that he had made his prearrangements elsewhere.

You see the point. It burned this man up to have his name miscalled and more importantly to be regarded with such apparent disrespect when he was there to bring business to the funeral home. His reaction was not petty; it was very human. Being self-centered, we unconsciously expect others to accord us, and our name, deference and respect.

HOW TO REMEMBER NAMES

The old saying that "business is sensitive—it goes where it is welcomed and stays where it is well treated" is so because human beings are sensitive. We *all* look for friendliness and goodwill, and we appreciate it when people use our names correctly.

Some of us have difficulty in remembering names because we have not tried to cultivate the habit. The habit *can* be cultivated. You may not care to use this system, but years ago James J. Hill, the great railroad builder, invented for his use a system for remembering names.

To a friend who inquired about this system, Mr. Hill replied, "As soon as I meet a person whose name I feel I should remember, I say to them, as we part company, 'Now, I want to be sure to remember your name right. The first initial is F, isn't it? The second is L, right? And your last name is spelled M-O-S-I-E-R correct?' Upon his departure, I first print the name out F. L. Mosier. Then, I write it the way it sounds, like this—EFF ELL MOSHUR—at the same time, thinking of some individual characteristics of the person—black, straight hair; deep-set blue eyes; cleft chin; some particular thing about the person's appearance; or even their manner of talking or walking—something distinctly individual to that person. In the course of a week, I may have a collection of 50 names thus analyzed, keeping them on little strips of paper. After dinner, some nights, I review these names, mentally calling off the person each one represents to me. You would be surprised how fascinating this game becomes in a short while."

Here is another easy remembering method. Take the name "James J. Hill," for instance. Think of that name as two jaybirds sitting on a hill. You'll remember it!

You dignify the client and bind their patronage more closely to your funeral home. You definitely increase your value, and you add to your own popularity and efficiency by getting the names right.

Regard a name with the same care you would treat the human being possessing it, for our name is a living part of us. When it comes to our name, we all bruise easily.

THE OTHER PERSON

The other person's name is, to that person, the most important name in the world. Respect it. Get it right, use it right, remember it, and don't nick it with a nickname. Getting a name right helps get you in right with its owner. This is important in winning friends and clients for your business.

 ## DISCUSSION QUESTIONS

1. Make a list of as many full names as you can and explain how you remembered them.

2. Tell how you have been embarrassed when your own name was mispronounced.

3. How do you respond when people are too familiar?

4. Explain your system for remembering names.

28

THE VALUE OF LISTENING

"Listen with care. It is so easy to break eggs without
making omelettes."

C. S. Lewis

 LEARNING OBJECTIVES

- Communicate the value of listening.

- Understand how challenging effective listening can be.

- Explain the relationship between good listening and complaint handling.

- Exhibit the skill of using interested listening, and memorize the twelve techniques to improved listening.

TWO MARVELOUS GIFTS

The human ear is a marvelous organ. In its intricate construction lies the priceless gift of hearing. By means of it, the brain is enabled to catch impressions and information so vital to success, happiness, and physical well-being.

But many blessed with hearing lack the ability of *listening!* Many of us choose to air *our* views, *our* ideas, *our* desires, *our* aims, and *our* virtues, rather than listen to the other fellow. Thus, we not only reduce our opportunities to learn, but we fail to use the strategy of listening which so effectively wins client goodwill.

Being a listener is really not difficult. It simply means that a person stops talking and starts hearing. Being an *effective listener* is difficult and requires intentional discipline and practice.

When you listen intently, it pleases the speaker and invites his confidence. He feels that you appreciate his words and that you have discriminating judgment. He is encouraged to tell you more. As all funeral professionals who make arrangements can attest, the habit of listening builds goodwill and generates valuable information.

THE LISTENING ATTITUDE PLEASES

I once worked for a funeral director who was an outstanding listener. One evening, during a wake, a man came up and started to talk the arm off this funeral director. I stood by and watched the whole scenario play out.

Eventually, the talkative man ran out of steam, and my employer thanked the man and went about his business. A few minutes later, the talkative man came up to me and said, "Your boss—wow, he sure is an intelligent man." I asked, "Why? He didn't say a dozen words to you." The man replied, "Well, he listened to me talk, didn't he? That's why I think your boss is a smart man."

It is a strange quirk in human vanity that causes the speaker to like a good listener. At times, we are all bored by some long-winded talker who imagines we are captivated by his words or voice. There is some compensation in listening even to a bore. He likes us for our attentiveness and thinks we're "smart."

"I'M TELLING YOU!"

It is amusing to observe the tendency in others to do all the talking, how they can scarcely wait for the chance to cut in with their voice, and how impatiently they listen! Notice how often "I'm telling you" occurs in the average conversation. Yes, there are people who have egos that make it difficult for them to use their ears more and their mouths less, but this type of egotism has no place in a helping profession like funeral service.

How often have you been exasperated by someone's failure to get your instructions right? Did the staff member listen to you carefully? Probably not. Think of mistakes that have occurred in funeral homes every day because people just don't listen. Valuable messages, important instructions, and requests go in one ear and out the other. In the funeral profession, this carelessness in listening is very dangerous.

CLIENTS OUT-TALKED OFTEN WALK OUT

A client will often refuse to transact with anyone who will not listen to what he or she wants to discuss. Permitting the client to give open expression to his wants or opinions enables every funeral professional to know how to better serve and create satisfaction.

When I first started to present caskets, I was mostly concerned with memorizing the assortment that we offered and the scripts I had regarding the different merits of each casket.

One day, I was presenting the caskets to a single lady and I was going on and on. Little did I realize that she was trying in vain to ask me a question. And little did I know that my employer was listening in, unseen, hearing all of my verbiage.

Finally, my employer stepped in and greeted the lady. She literally gasped with relief. "I know you'll answer the question

I've been trying to ask for the last twenty minutes!" I could have died, and my employer took over, much to the gratification of the lady.

Later, I did a lot of wholehearted listening to my boss concerning the art of listening. He asked me to seriously study my own style and reactions. Didn't I warm up to the person who listened to me with interest? Didn't I respect and like my associates who listened to me? This funeral director was absolutely right, and my listening to him helped me avoid future errors and increased my effectiveness as a funeral director.

LISTENING: A SAFETY VALVE FOR COMPLAINTS

A friend of mine owns a large and very reputable funeral home in a Western city. Over the door of the staff lounge is a sign that reads: "The knowledge of when to keep silent is golden." On his staff, he has identified two people, one a man and the other a woman, who serve as his "listeners" to complaints, taking the motto to heart!

Experience has taught this wise funeral director that the quickest way to settle complaints agreeably is to lend a friendly, attentive ear. His listeners are instructed to answer calls in this manner: "Hello, Mrs. Jones, this is Bill Bowe." "Hello, Mrs. Johnson, this is Mary Shoemaker."

The complaining client is usually disarmed by these friendly sounding voices and the kind attitude that accompanies them. Then, the listening starts. As the criticism goes on, the listener replies with a gentle "yes" or "is that so?." These listeners let the client get a complaint out of his or her system, and 80 percent of the time what started out to be a client changing loyalty away from the funeral home ends up to be a loyal, re-established, satisfied client. The funeral director believes that his listeners are worth thousands of dollars a year in the loyalty of clients saved.

IT MUST BE INTERESTED LISTENING

Important as it is to listen, it is equally important to listen with real interest. You can develop the habit of being really interested when you regard the words of a client as being the "pay" for your funeral career. There is much you can mentally discard, but here and there will be a golden gem of information worth storing away in your memory. Pretending interest you don't feel is as bad as not listening at all. The other person senses whether your attention is on the level, and *nowhere* is this more true than a funeral arrangement conference.

The famous Supreme Court Justice and great thinker, Oliver Wendell Holmes, Jr., once wrote these words to a brash, aspiring, young politician:

> To be able to listen to others in a sympathetic and understanding manner is perhaps the most effective mechanism in the world for getting along with people and tying up their friendship for good. Too few people practice the magic of being a good listener.

What you want to say, what you want to do, what your troubles are, and how you gain some advantage are not important *all the time* to the other person. The personal pronouns "I," "me," and "mine" in relation to a client are the ones that the client is most interested in. Remembering this in our funeral careers can give us a great insight in listening. Always remember: The other person's voice and the other person's story may be the voice of opportunity for *you!*

TWELVE TECHNIQUES TO IMPROVE LISTENING

1. Shut up! This may sound a little blunt, but no one can talk and listen at the same time.
2. Recognize that listening is something you do for personal success.
3. You must *want* to listen better.
4. Work on becoming less self-centered.
5. Prepare to listen.
6. Work hard at listening.
7. Check for nonverbal cues.
8. Hold your fire—don't interrupt.
9. Don't plan your response while the person is talking.
10. Overcome distractions.
11. When you need to hear *everything* a person is saying, say to yourself, "Right now, understanding this person's feelings is more important than understanding *everything* he or she is saying."
12. Practice making the decisions you need to make about people and events without coming to final conclusions about them.

DISCUSSION QUESTIONS

1. How do you describe effective listening?

2. Why is good listening such a powerful tool?

3. How can we improve our listening skills?

4. How can we discreetly shift conversations with clients who are getting long-winded?

29

CONFIDENCE IN FUNERAL SERVICE

Know What You Are Talking About

"Society is built on trust, and trust upon confidence in one another's integrity."

Robert South

 LEARNING OBJECTIVES

- Understand that no one likes guesses.

- Explain the idea: *no knowledge equals no power.*

- Compare and contrast respect with families and your own knowledge base.

- Explain the concept of gentle confidence.

NO ONE LIKES TO TRUST GUESSES

It is inspiring to hear a dynamic speaker or professional person whose word we can confidently accept. On the other hand, it is depressing to hear someone "talking big" about something he or she knows little about. In the funeral service profession, to talk without complete knowledge of the facts is dangerous ground, and it exposes one to ridicule and contempt.

It is not only bad form to try to impress someone with our superior knowledge, but it can be disastrous in funeral service, particularly if we are only guessing—or worse, bluffing. We invite scorn and complaints from families when they act on information that we have given them which is inaccurate or completely false, thus causing trouble or inconvenience.

The safe plan in funeral service is to tell no more than you know to be fact. When you state facts, you never have to remember what you say.

NO KNOWLEDGE EQUALS NO POWER

A pre-need saleswoman was being secretly videotaped during a sales presentation. At the conclusion of the session, the family member objected to buying a container to put the cremated remains in. The pre-need saleswoman said, "It is required." The family member asked, "Is it state law?" "Yes" was the response from the saleswoman.

The fact was the state had *no laws* concerning cremain containers. The transaction made national news and all because the saleswoman had no knowledge of her own state laws! It was embarrassing and terribly humiliating, but nonetheless it was the saleswoman's own fault. She should have had the facts.

No matter what we present—be it compassion, an idea, a suggestion, a casket, a service option, or an embalmed body—get and give complete information. When you are informed, you have a sense of power that knowledge brings.

Even the fact of trying to learn is a profitable step toward advancement. Thomas A. Edison, inventive genius that he was, once said: "I am no genius. I am merely inquisitive. There is no limit to the number of things I want to know."

FUNERAL PROFESSIONAL MADE SURE HE WAS RIGHT

A highly successful funeral director once relayed his formula for success. He monitored and solicited from his families how they reacted to and commented on the embalming his firm did.

He kept track of all the positive and negative comments. Then, he would compile this data and eventually he *knew* what type of body would receive the best comments, and he also *knew* who did the best work and which chemicals and cosmetics were most satisfactory. The moral of the story is the types of body presentation his families liked best was not how he had originally wanted his embalming done. He had the confidence to abandon his old subjective ideas and went on to a highly successful career due mainly to the outstanding work that was accomplished in his preparation room. He knew what his community wanted!

ONE WAY TO WIN RESPECT OF FAMILIES

When you speak with authority, backed by knowledge of your subject, you command the respect of your families and your associates.

A young man whose wife had just died sat in the funeral home office. The funeral director was very experienced, and when the subject of the monument came up, the young man stated firmly that he wanted both names engraved on the stone because "they would be together forever." This wise funeral director, based on his experiential knowledge, looked at the young man and said, "We can certainly do that, but here is a thought—why not, for the time being, just engrave your wife's name on the stone. Then, later we can add yours." The young man looked upset, "I want both names engraved!" he exclaimed. The funeral director leaned over and gently said, "I know, but you are a young man, and if you remarry, all those plans could change very much. We will do what you wish, but think about it."

The young man thought and eventually agreed with the funeral director. The gentle confidence and wisdom of the funeral director had avoided a future awkward situation.

This happened in 1930, and the man did eventually remarry. His second marriage lasted over 40 years and as he aged, his wish was to be buried next to his second wife. This man always thanked that funeral director for sharing his knowledge that fateful day and saving him from doing something that he would later regret.

THE SATISFACTION OF KNOWING

You save yourself embarrassment and trouble when you are able to render service, knowledge, and suggestions confidently and accurately. Then, there can be no complaints, no kickbacks to your funeral home, and no needless adjustments or possible loss.

As a funeral professional, when you know what you are talking about, the family is usually aware of this fact. It is an important way to win the respect and cooperation of others.

DISCUSSION QUESTIONS

1. What can be the consequences of guessing at an answer?

2. What are the areas related to your profession where you could use more knowledge?

3. How can we gain more knowledge in such areas?

4. When you don't know the real answer to a question, what do you usually do and say?

FUNERAL PROFESSIONALS ARE ALWAYS DIPLOMATS

"There is nothing so strong as gentleness, and there is nothing so gentle as real strength."

St. Francis de Sales

LEARNING OBJECTIVES

- Know the definition of an *everyday diplomat*.
- Explain the risk factor of being undiplomatic with a family.
- Explain the first step in funeral diplomacy.
- Define the term *squawk suppressor*.

DIPLOMACY INCREASES YOUR VALUE

During the administration of Canada's Prime Minister Sir Robert Laird Borden, a diplomatic crisis arose which had the Canadian Parliament on edge. The Prime Minister, however, refused to be disturbed by it. During the so-called crisis, he said at an advisor's meeting, "You gentlemen are taking this thing too seriously. I'll wager a good clerk from any department store in town could settle this thing amicably in twenty minutes.

"What we need in this case is an 'everyday diplomat' instead of high-flown, beating-around-the-bush diplomacy. I'll tell you, gentlemen, there is more commonsense, practical diplomacy practiced in business than in all the ambassadorial circles in the world put together."

While Borden made this statement many years ago, it is as true today as it was the day he said it. In fact, his statement was a splendid compliment to people in business life. It is the practice of everyday diplomacy that makes the wheels of the business world go around with a minimum of friction, particularly in the funeral service profession.

Those who become proficient in this practical art are far more valuable, have more friends, and reap richer rewards than those who cannot handle the difficult situations that arise every day or who use the take-no-prisoners attitude in dealing with rough waters.

A POLICY THAT WINS FAMILIES

A funeral director in Boston, who is regarded throughout the profession as an outstanding professional, operates under the philosophy of daily diplomacy. Behind his success are his policies for handling families. One of these is that in case of a complaint from a family, the funeral director graciously concedes that the family is right and must receive satisfaction both emotionally and financially. This policy of diplomacy has no doubt cost this funeral director thousands, but it has earned his company millions.

Apply this strategy to your own career. Admit your mistakes. Even if you are right 99 times out of 100, your family will honestly believe they were right too. Maybe you can convince them you were right and they were wrong, but you will greatly risk losing a family for yourself and your funeral home. Diplomatically, give the family break. That is part of everyday diplomacy.

THE FIRST STEP IN FUNERAL DIPLOMACY

Why should there be friction between our families and ourselves? The answer is clear. The family thinks, "We are spending hard-earned money, and we insist on full value and consideration!" In nearly every case of customer friction, something pretty close to "pocketbook logic" is behind it. Thus, sympathetic consideration of the family's point of view is the first step in successful, diplomatic dealing with that family.

Occasionally, something besides pocketbook logic is behind a family's complaint. In Nashville several years ago, a funeral director served a family who insisted that the funeral flowers be ordered through a florist that the funeral director knew had a terrible reputation. The funeral director tried to gently persuade the family to use a highly reputable florist, but they would hear nothing of the sort.

When the flowers arrived, the funeral director knew that he had been right. The flowers were dead. He immediately called the reputable florist and had an identical spray sent over. When the family arrived, the funeral director explained what had happened and let the family see the original casket spray. The funeral director could see that they were embarrassed, so he gave them a break by saying, "I knew you would be dissatisfied once you saw the original spray. The new one is beautiful and cost $10.00 less. Let's go look at it."

The family raved about the spray, and the funeral director made his point very diplomatically without damaging the family's dignity. So diplomatically did this funeral director handle this situation that the family sent him over 20 funerals throughout his career.

The good feeling that a generous, diplomatic attitude generates often results in a desire on the part of a client to give you more business, as in this funeral director's case.

DIPLOMACY IS EASIER ON THE NERVES

The everyday diplomat in funeral service is invariably popular with families and fellow employees alike. His or her tactfulness is inspiring and has a calming effect on those inclined to flare up and "get huffy."

"THE SQUAWK SUPPRESSOR"

A large funeral home in New York City does over 3,000 funerals a year and has no parking except curbside—not one parking space. What they do have is a valet that is nicknamed "the squawk suppressor."

When a person pulls up in front of the funeral home, the squawk suppressor is right there. "May I help you?" "There's no place to park—what's with this place?" "You're right," the squawk suppressor replies, "but don't worry about it, I'll take care of it."

With that, the valet opens the car door and whisks the car around the corner. He chauffeurs cars all day long and keeps people happy. In addition, he always sides with the client.

DIPLOMACY CREATES FRIENDS

Over the years, this valet, "the squawk suppressor," has made thousands of friends. In fact, the manager of the funeral home attributes the firm's continually high volume, in a tightly crowded metropolitan area, in part, to the professional diplomacy of the valet.

HOW YOU PROFIT

For the sake of your own success and progress, practice being an everyday diplomat. You cannot help profiting, while at the same time increasing your happiness, popularity, and usefulness.

DISCUSSION QUESTIONS

1. Describe an *everyday diplomat.* Does this describe you?

2. How does the use of diplomacy deal with *pocketbook logic?*

3. Are there areas of your funeral home in which you need a *squawk suppressor?*

4. Think of an instant where you exercised diplomacy. Perhaps you knew you were right, but did you let the client be right?

31

TACT

*"If we lose affection and kindliness from our life, we lose all that
gives it charm."*

Cicero

LEARNING OBJECTIVES

- Articulate why the consideration of others' feelings is essential in funeral service.

- Understand how tact can rescue people from awkward situations.

- Appreciate and explain how tact is always mindful of the other person's interests.

- Explain the relationship of tact and a sense of humor.

CONSIDERATION FOR THE FEELINGS OF OTHERS

Tactfulness is the very essence of getting along successfully with others. Its daily practice is vitally important to everyone in the funeral home, particularly to those who serve families. The meaning of tact, from a funeral service perspective, is not entirely clear to many, and it is well that it be defined anew: "Tact is consideration of the feelings of others. It is a subtle form of courtesy and thoughtfulness that enables one to do and say the right thing under all circumstances."

TACT FORESTALLS ARGUMENT

Funeral directors are a noble group of people. They have impeccable reputations in their communities for dependability, dignity, and tact.

A few years ago, a funeral director from Minneapolis was serving on a hospital board of directors. The hospital needed to greatly increase the amount of money contributed by the Minneapolis business community for a major fund-raising effort.

The funeral director was in charge of the fund-raising effort. Had he said to the business community, "The board decided you've got to kick in with a lot more money this year," he would have met only resistance and refusal. Fortunately, he knew it.

Tactfully, therefore, he put himself on the side of the business community. The hospital board, he told them, hoped to triple contributions, but he was opposed to the plan. "I believe we should only double the contribution," he said, "not triple it."

The funeral director was given hearty applause from the business community. He was on their side, trying to save them money. Their checks, for double the amount of their previous year's contributions, poured in.

CONSIDERATION WINS THE DAY

A lady could not decide on her mother's casket. She came back and forth to the funeral home five times, spent a couple of hours at each attempt, and left in frustration. Embarrassed, the lady told the funeral director: "I hate to be so indecisive, but I want this to be right."

The funeral director tactfully replied: "Oh, you must not feel that way. I don't want you to purchase anything that is not right for you. After all, you must be satisfied, and that is not a little thing with you or with me. I have told you everything I can concerning the construction and value of these caskets. My job is to serve you the best way that I can. If this funeral home didn't have great people like you, I'd be out of a job."

Tact came to the rescue. A touchy matter had been disposed of with increased good feeling instead of ill will. Importantly, that funeral director had tactfully explained the true status of the funeral service profession, namely, that families deserve and must have full value and satisfaction for the money they spend. Families appreciate such understanding in a funeral professional.

TACT IS KINDLY AND INOFFENSIVE

Another great element in the practice of tactfulness is the ability to never offend in any manner.

An executive director of a very successful funeral service association once explained his formula for the great success of his state's convention and meeting. His basic idea was to understand the funeral director's mind well enough so that everything planned would be in line with expectations and needs. He made sure that the speakers' handouts and information were also appropriate, and would compliment, empower, and promote the value of the funeral.

At these conventions, the tactful message to the funeral director was "look at what you do right," versus "look at what you do wrong." His meetings and conventions were sell-outs—and no wonder; if you were going to pay money to attend, which type of meeting would most attract you?

TACT IS MINDFUL OF THE OTHER'S INTERESTS

It is always good to remember in dealing with another person that, regardless of their temperament, they are most interested in themselves, and any remark or action on our part that honors or serves them is the quickest road to goodwill.

I once knew a funeral director who was particularly fond of babies. Whenever a doting mother would proudly exhibit her baby, this funeral director always exclaimed admiringly, "Well, that *is* a baby!" The remark saved a lot of useless babble. It was a tactful, well-rounding phrase and always made a hit with mothers. Whatever we do or say is apt to be on the safe side if prompted by a kind or complimentary thought.

Those dealing directly with families must, of course, adapt themselves to varying temperaments, and tact is constantly required. The nervous, impatient client wants quick action. Give it to him. The slow, methodical person often strains one's patience, but we must tactfully adapt our pace to his too. There are, of course, many other types of people, and they must all be handled with tactful appreciation of their problems.

HIS TACT SAVED HIM FROM EMBARRASSMENT

When a leading funeral director in a small Ohio community ran for mayor, he polled so few votes that he realized he would be the laughing stock of the town. His social and business standing were in danger, for it is hard to hold one's ground when everyone is laughing. The funeral director was savvy enough to realize his predicament and tactful enough to take his defeat like a good sport.

The next morning, after the election's outcome was known, townsfolk passing his funeral home saw a sign that read: "$25.00 reward for the name of the person who cast that vote for me."

When people saw the sign, they laughed *with* the funeral director, not *at* him. At visitations and funerals, they congratulated him on his good sportsmanship. His stinging defeat might have aroused his anger and soured him, but tact and a little humor in handling a difficult situation brought that funeral director even more attention and more respect than he had enjoyed before.

For funeral professionals, tactfulness is an outward indication of an inward consideration for the other person. They smooth their own path by smoothing the path for others. This process constantly creates new friends, and everyone recognizes a superior person.

DISCUSSION QUESTIONS

1. What is tact? How does it contribute to goodwill?

2. How does one "see the other side" and use that skill to their advantage?

3. Describe some scenarios where tact would come in handy. Briefly role play.

4. Talk about the variety of personalities you have handled in the last year. Which ones required extra tact?

32

WHAT IMPRESSION DO YOU CREATE?

"Never trust your tongue when your heart is better."

Samuel J. Harwitt

LEARNING OBJECTIVES

- Understand that all bereaved persons have sharp eyes to detect insincerities.

- Explain what the term *bond of faith* means.

- Understand how friendliness and sincerity help funeral directors.

- Explain and understand the moral behind the story of President Lincoln's mole.

O. Henry, the master short-story writer, told of a young man working in a train depot, who regularly saved and stinted so that one night out of ninety, he could rent formal attire and dine out like a millionaire. As he started out on one of these special occasions, he encountered a plainly dressed girl who had sprained her ankle on the street corner. Gallantly assisting her, he invited her to dine with him while resting her ankle.

He ordered an elaborate dinner and talked airily of the Parker House in Boston and the Palmer House in Chicago, intimated a yacht lying off Bar Harbor, and spoke knowingly of the "season" on the Riviera. He put on what he considered a stellar performance and was quite pleased with himself.

Having dined and rested her ankle sufficiently to bear her

weight, the girl thanked him and left. She walked toward the entrance of a magnificent townhouse on Park Avenue and took out her key and walked in. Her older sister, regally dressed, greeted her, "Sis, where have you been? Father has been frantic, and he even sent the chauffeur out looking for you." Quickly explaining the mishap, the young girl then said with a sigh, "Sis, do you suppose we will ever meet somebody who is interested in something besides their yachts and Bar Harbor and just having a good time? Does Papa's wealth keep us from ever knowing a person who is truly of an authentic character with a noble purpose in life?"

You get the point. That young man's four-flushing front actually ruined what might have been. In the funeral profession, a fake front can just as easily turn to one's own disadvantage. We have all seen, and no doubt experienced, the sight of people putting on an act, trying to be other than their own natural selves. Sometimes, it is of political necessity to act and behave a certain way, a matter of etiquette and formality. That is not what we are talking about. We're talking about putting on an act that is no more convincing than the fake "dickies" that people wear to give the impression they are wearing a fine, expensive sweater.

THE BEREAVED HAVE SHARP EYES THAT SEE THROUGH THE VENEER

Pretenders like this in funeral service are fooling only themselves. Families sense whether you are on the level. They can tell whether you are indifferent or genuinely have their interests at heart, or whether you are building yourself up for some alternative advantage. When our attitude toward them is warm and friendly, it can only react in our favor.

Everyone wants to make a favorable impression, to appear capable and to always outshine the funeral home down the street. Yet, some of us know our own deficiencies. To cover them up, we often try to be what we really aren't, which is a mistake. The funeral professional who lends a helping hand at every opportunity just for the joy of doing so never has to put on an act. Nothing invites authentic admiration or goodwill quicker than being thoughtful of others.

BONDS OF FAITH

A funeral director who had a tremendous number of full-service funerals was asked by his boss what his secret was. "I don't know," he said, "I just believe in the value of the funeral so strongly, I guess people believe me." His families could feel his confidence and sincerity. They knew he was right.

A casket company representative was once asked who he liked to call on best. "Big funeral directors," he answered. "The big director is usually the one who always takes the time to hear my story and gives it his sincere attention. He is big, not in size or volume, but because he is willing to learn my story. They are the genuine ones."

While common sense tells us to be sincere, it does not mean we must be perfectly frank at all times. The person who tells you frankly just what is wrong with you—your clothes, your hair style, or your ability—secretly antagonizes rather than helps. The best impression is tact, courtesy, and kindness.

POPULAR WITH FAMILIES

Natural friendliness wins hosts of friends. A funeral director's office in the Midwest is the social center of the town. Friends just drop in for a moment's chat whenever they can. He even has cards that they send him when they are abroad on business or pleasure.

A funeral home in the Southwest has a funeral director who is the soul of friendliness and sincerity. "Everyone wants Carlos to wait on them," the funeral home manager said, "and I don't blame them. He simply radiates warm, friendly kindness that makes our families his friends." The point is that Carlos is not faking it. He is naturally solicitive and eager to please, and families react to him as they always react to the genuine article.

A funeral home always reflects the mental attitude of the people in it. Families are sensitive to an atmosphere of sincerity and goodwill or to its opposite.

The most sincere kind of practical advice is: Don't put on an act. The poses may get by for a time, but eventually problems wait for them around the corner.

THE MOLE

A portrait painter said to Abraham Lincoln, "Do you want me to paint that big mole on your face or leave it off, Mr. President?" The President replied, "If that mole isn't there, it won't be Lincoln."

DISCUSSION QUESTIONS

1. How would you define a sincere impression?

2. Do you know of any families who have seen through a personality veneer?

3. Give some examples of how you have become popular with families?

4. How do you feel when people put on an act?

33

WHY ARGUE?

LEARNING OBJECTIVES

- Understand how arguing creates the reverse in making friends.

- Explain why it is valuable to get the other person's viewpoint.

- Know how a generous attitude diffuses most arguments.

- Be able to explain why having your ego under control helps you win goodwill and friendship.

Everyone in funeral service wants to be liked; we all want friends. In this profession, given the negative media treatment *it is essential* to be well thought of by everyone. To win a friend, you wouldn't say, "Your opinion doesn't count with me. Let me tell you how smart I am. I can show you how wrong you are and how right I am. Don't talk, I'm not interested in what you say—just listen to me!"

Can you imagine anyone's being attracted by that attitude? In effect, this is often just what we are saying when we argue, no matter what words we use. In spite of all the evidence that arguing results only in harm, many of us permit ourselves to be drawn into its deadly trap. People who win arguments think they have won, but it is usually an illusion.

FRIENDSHIP IN "REVERSE"

No matter what your role in the funeral home, your success depends on your ability to get along with everyone. As a funeral professional, you may not think of yourself as a salesperson in the usual sense, but you must "sell" yourself and goodwill on your job in order to keep things running smoothly.

You may silence your fellow funeral home workers by arguing, but you probably will not cause a change of mind, except they may resent you even more. A person who argues from a position of superiority usually is very mean and cruel in tactics. This person will ridicule the other person's lack of knowledge, causing embarrassment and resentment. This applies to everyone from the manager of the funeral home to the gardener and the apprentice.

WE CANNOT AND DO NOT ARGUE GOODWILL INTO ANYONE

People are attracted to you because you compliment, are courteous and respectful, and go out of your way, if necessary, to please them. By arguing, you simply advertise to the other person that you value yourself more highly than you do anyone else. You will eventually lose confidence, cooperation, and goodwill.

GET THE OTHER PERSON'S VIEWPOINT

When anyone wants to argue, just remember that you want that person's goodwill. Why does he want to argue? Well, maybe he's in a difficult mood. Maybe he wants to impress you with his knowledge, or maybe he is of the opinion that he must *always* be right. All right, let him have his way. It doesn't hurt to listen. We learn by listening. Some people want to impress. All right, be impressed. It usually pleases people to think that others value their ideas. So do it—they'll like you for it. You may not mentally agree with the position, but be a sympathetic and attentive listener. You will find an opportunity to state some facts of your own, calmly and pleasantly. Because you refuse to argue, you will gain respect.

FRANKLIN WAS NOT A BORN DIPLOMAT

Benjamin Franklin was not a born diplomat, but by watching the art of diplomacy in others, he developed a grand style of grace and dignity.

As a young man, Franklin was cocksure, self-important, and liked to argue until one day an older man said to him, "Your opinions have a slap in them for everyone who differs from you. No one cares to hear them. Your friends find they enjoy themselves better when you are not around." From that day on, Franklin studied how to avoid antagonizing. Getting the other person's viewpoint was the key to an understanding of human nature that ultimately made him a master diplomat.

IF YOU DON'T ARGUE, NO ONE CAN ARGUE WITH YOU

The attitude displayed in our funeral homes and towards our friends is unconsciously taken with us everywhere. If we avoid arguing with members of our staff, family, and friends, we are certain to be tactful and pleasing in our professional contacts.

Arguing in a funeral home usually creates confusion, resulting in serious disadvantages to the firm and particularly to our families. Arguing stirs ill will, and ill will breeds carelessness, indifference, and costly mistakes. Businesses of all kinds lose heavily because the men and women in it, whose work brings them into contact with the public, often antagonize families by arguing.

No matter what your role in the funeral home may be, listen attentively. Show consideration for the other person's point of view. Show that you are open-minded, willing to learn, and interested in hearing him. It is a winning way. Make a statement of facts in a way that does not suggest you are forcing your point of view on your listener but that you offer the thought only for consideration.

When you have finished talking, let it be with an air of pleasant finality. Calmly present your facts, then let the other person act accordingly. If he or she still persists in wanting to argue, say nothing. You cannot argue with silence, and no one ever got into trouble by keeping silent.

A GENEROUS ATTITUDE SHAMES ARGUMENTS

Here is how a great-uncle of mine refused to argue and won the goodwill of a customer who wanted to argue. The work of the funeral home may bear no relation whatsoever to that of my uncle's work, but you will get the point.

My uncle operated an implement company in the Midwest and he sold stoves wholesale to distributors. A dealer ordered an oil cooking stove. Upon its arrival, he wrote a burning letter of complaint to my uncle's company. *"There were no legs for the stove . . ."* After checking carefully, one of my uncle's employees found that the stove had positively been shipped complete. However, my uncle avoided an argument. He shipped an additional set of legs with the following letter:

> Dear Mr. Adams:
> We regret our recent incomplete shipment to you. Permit me to send you another set of stove legs.

Then he added a postscript:

> Have you looked in the oven?

The new set of legs and the letter arrived simultaneously. Mr. Adams looked in the oven, and sure enough, there were the "lost" legs. His face was no doubt very red. He returned the extra set without comment. Within a few weeks, however, he wrote my uncle and ordered four more stoves.

My uncle was a wise man and had his ego well under control. Knowing the customer would argue heatedly for his "rights," whether right or wrong, he didn't propose to create ill will for his firm or himself. He refused to argue. His generous assumption that the customer was right (plus the way he chose to bring out the facts) saved the customer's dignity and won his active goodwill. We can exercise the same good sense in our contact with everyone in the funeral home, with families, and with everyone else.

A THOUGHT FOR EACH MORNING

"Today, I will have to deal with many people who like to argue, but who do not like to be opposed by arguments. I must substitute skillful handling of each case for my natural desire to fight back." Even if you win an argument, the other person can beat you every time by refusing to cooperate with you or by refusing to deal with your funeral home—or worse, by influencing others not to deal with your firm or with you.

It is true that you cannot win by arguing, so *why argue?*

DISCUSSION QUESTIONS

1. Give examples of situations in which you argued. What was the outcome?

2. How do you feel when people argue with you?

3. Have you ever lost a friend over an argument?

4. What ways have you developed to deal with arguments?

34

THE ART OF PERSUASION

"He, from whose lips divine persuasion flows."

Alexander Pope

 LEARNING OBJECTIVES

- Understand the safe way to influence people.

- Articulate the risks of commanding people.

- Understand the relationship between persuasion and politeness.

- Explain the concept of the power of persuasion.

HOW TO INFLUENCE PEOPLE

The cheap ballyhoo of the ordinary "carnival barker" offers a glaring example of how *not* to persuade. He makes the mistake of assuming that his audience is unintelligent—will swallow his exaggerated statements, fake enthusiasm, and lack of restraint—and can be forced and herded into action.

Human nature resents being bossed, or being taken for easy marks. When we do something for someone, we like to think that we are doing so voluntarily. Yet, many of us, in spite of the fact that we do not like to be driven, often antagonize others and disrupt friendships by thoughtlessly trying to force them instead of using persuasion and retaining their goodwill.

The essence of persuasion is getting a person to want to do what you suggest. Human nature always does best what it wants to do. That should be remembered in your contacts at the funeral home.

ASKED—NEVER COMMANDED

An influential funeral director in Idaho is well respected and affectionately regarded by his entire staff. They like his way of handling them. He is a master in what is termed *the gentle art of persuasion.*

He never gives direct orders. When he wants something done, it's "Joe, will you do so-and-so for me?" or "Sarah, I'd like to have such-and-such fixed up—will you take care of it for me?" He always has that dignified, respectful attitude toward his associates that makes them feel independent. His pleasant persuasion makes them glad to serve; it makes them feel that they are performing the service voluntarily. They would go through hell and high water to make good with that "boss."

A FUNDAMENTAL RULE IN HUMAN RELATIONS

It is a well-known fact in psychology that only lower mental capabilities respond to an absolute command. Healthy minds resent the direct order but always respond better to the persuasive suggestion. Never say "Do this or do that." Instead say, "When you do this or that, this or that will result to your advantage."

THEY FOLLOWED THE SUGGESTION

My grandfather owned three large farms in the Midwest. During the Depression, he lost his workers, and with the harvest only weeks off, he was in a real jam. Unable to hire labor at any cost, he could not decide which farm to concentrate on because it was obvious that he was going to have to do the work himself. One night, he went into town and got three newcomers into a corner of the general store and suggested: "Boys, I'm going to do you a favor. I know you can use some easy money. I have three farms and I need help in the harvest. I can't pay you now, but I'll give you one fourth of the proceeds to split three ways."

The three men jumped at the chance. My grandfather had persuaded these men to do the very job he could not afford to *hire* out.

"WHAT'S IN IT FOR ME?"

Persuasion is far more than just saying, "Won't you please do so-and-so for me?" This is a selfish request. The other person's natural reaction is, "Do it for you? Say, what's in it for me?" Of course, it is only common politeness to ask someone to do something rather than order them to do it. But persuasion goes deeper than politeness.

THE POWER OF HER PERSUASION

One day a woman rang the doorbell at the funeral home I managed. She told me she was out of a job and wanted work. She had heard through the grapevine that it was difficult for women to get a job in a funeral home, but she assured me she was truly interested in the profession.

She received an interview with the owner, who had a very limited view of a woman's role in funeral service. He came up with every possible objection, but she pitted her persuasiveness and came back at him every time.

She admitted her limited background and the fact that her other job probably did not prepare her for funeral work. She admitted that she was not licensed but emphasized and focused on her deep interest in this profession.

Most of all, her vision shone through. Her enthusiasm was contagious. She had ideas of what she could contribute to the funeral home. Reluctantly, my boss hired her. That was in 1977. Today, she owns her own funeral home.

To go through life with a minimum of friction and constantly enjoy the cooperation of others is the wish of every normal human being. Persuasion is the key to that happy state, and persuasion has its beginning in the right mental attitude toward others. Hold their interests in mind, and your suggestions will have power.

DISCUSSION QUESTIONS

1. Describe a person you know who is persuasive.

2. Describe a life experience when you were persuasive.

3. Discuss the differences in how Lincoln persuaded people versus how Adolf Hitler persuaded people.

4. How do you respond to a persuasive person?

35

COMMUNICATION BLUNDERS

"Better to throw a stone at random than a word."

Pope Xystus I

LEARNING OBJECTIVES

- Understand and explain the concept of "watch your words."

- Explain why belittling, flip answers are so dangerous.

- Define these types of communication blunders: the "Bore," the "Questioner," the "Blusterer," the "Loud Speaker," and the "Disputer."

- Explain the value of "be bright, be brief, be gone."

WATCH YOUR WORDS

In an age when efficiency is being stressed and our inventive genius is producing every conceivable comfort, luxury, and advantage, it is amazing how little most of us devote to our style of communication and the words we use.

Many are particular about personal appearance and the environment of the cemetery and/or funeral home, yet thoughtlessly destroy the effect because of shabby language. "Shabby" talk is not confined to bad grammar or ill-chosen words. It includes those evidences of poor taste or downright ill nature that can earn the contempt of others.

The slogan "watch your step" has saved many lives. The slogan "watch your words" is one that everyone in our profession, particularly those dealing with families and the public, may well adopt. Conversational blunders are one of our worst betrayers.

THE MAKINGS OF POPULARITY

It seems that most of us talk too much, yet so much is better never said.

A successful embalming fluid representative in the Midwest was popular with all who knew him and was a perfect example of the wise old saying, "Be bright, be brief, be gone." No finer tribute could have been made of this man than what was written in his memorial folder at his own funeral:

> When you said goodbye to him, you felt better for having seen him. When he would make a suggestion to you, you never felt that he was criticizing. You would always come away from him with a lifted feeling. It was always a pleasure to be with him.

How many people do you know who fit that description? Many people are conversationally irritating. Consider the "interrupters," for instance. They never let you finish a sentence without butting in. They scarcely hear you, for they are too intent on what they want to say. If they would listen more, they would learn more; but their egos will never permit them to be courteous. In the funeral profession, these folks cause the family to see red.

BELITTLING

To belittle anyone is the surest way to earn their resentment. Just what a belittler thinks he or she gains by making one feel "cheap" is hard to figure. They are certainly not winning popularity nor admiration for their superior judgment or intellect!

I served two different apprenticeships in my training as a funeral director, and I well remember working under a funeral director who was a belittler. He would rant and rave at funerals and embarrass me directly in front of families. He always inferred that everyone else's judgment had been bad and that we wcrc all vcry lucky to havc somconc likc him around who rcally knew what funeral service was all about.

When the second hand on the clock tolled the end of my apprenticeship with this man, I was gone and vowed never to expose myself to such unleashed egotism again!

FLIP ANSWERS

Some people have the faculty of annoying others with their *flip-pancy*. Flippancy is saying more than the circumstances call for. Ask someone a question and instead of answering in a direct, businesslike way, he or she makes some unnecessary remarks to indicate "cleverness" or a sense (which is more often nonsense) of humor.

I remember a casket representative who, when asked how he was doing, would always respond with, "I was doing great until I saw you!" We bought very few caskets from this man.

THE "BORE"

Someone defined a bore as "a person who, when asked about his health, tells you!" The "Bore" is the king of conversational blunders. His pet subject is most often himself, and it is easy to start him off on it. That his listener may be bored to death never occurs to him. In the funeral profession, we need to steer clear of this type of person.

THE "QUESTIONER"

All funeral professionals expect a family to ask a lot of questions in order to ensure that they understand everything. In ordinary conversation, however, the person who cross-examines another out of idle curiosity had better watch his or her step. When people suspect the questioner of being "snoopy," he risks becoming an irritant, and this is precisely what we do not want to happen.

THE "BLUSTERER"

We are all acquainted with the "Blusterer." He is strong for *his* rights, but has no regard for the other person's. He also likes to brag. With him, it is always a case of "me and mine," and let "you and yours" take care of yourselves. Naturally, this person drives friends and families away from the funeral home.

THE "LOUD SPEAKER"

This person pulls out all the stops and takes everyone within a large radius into his "confidence." It makes no difference if he is embarrassing others. This person is in love with his own voice, and the louder he talks the better it sounds—to him!

One hot August day, a well-to-do woman drove her car into the service department of an automobile dealer because her air conditioner was broken. A month before, she had experienced a front-end collision so the fender was crumpled, the headlights were broken, and the grill was battered. When she got out of the car, she remarked to one of the men, "My, it's hot driving today." On noticing the wrecked front end, he bellowed, "Yeah, and I guess you're a hot driver, too." Adding insult to injury, he followed his broadcast with a hearty laugh and a wink to a group of customers waiting for their cars, but the customer didn't think it was funny. Neither did the service manager, who apologized for the rudeness, and placed a pink slip in the "Loud Speaker's" next pay envelope.

THE "DISPUTER"

The "Disputer" has his own niche in the hall of conversational blunders. The other person's comments are seldom correct. With his superior knowledge, the "Disputer" is always setting someone straight. The customer cannot be right because the "Disputer" knows all the answers himself. If the "Disputer" could look into the family's mind and see the contempt his attitude has created, he might not be so satisfied with himself.

As we read about these conversational blunders, it is natural to think, "Thank goodness I don't make them." Perhaps not, but read them again and seriously consider whether you do. "Watch your words" and watch how your popularity and efficiency grows.

 DISCUSSION QUESTIONS

1. Describe an experience when you said something wrong. What was the outcome?

2. Discuss the virtues of *not* interrupting.

3. How do you respond to flip answers?

4. Share an experience for each of the following types: the "Bore," the "Questioner," the "Blusterer," the "Loud Speaker," and the "Disputer."

V

COMMUNICATING
WITH FAMILIES

"Help thy brother's boat across, and lo! Thine own has reached the shore."

Hindu Proverb

36

MAKE IT EASIER FOR FAMILIES TO DEAL WITH YOU

"Bear ye one another's burdens, and so fulfill the law of Christ."

Galatians 6:2

 LEARNING OBJECTIVES

- Explain the concept of freedom of action.
- Understand the risks of judging others.
- Explain the canon of funeral service.
- Appreciate and respect the dangers of pressuring a family.

HUMAN NATURE DEMANDS FREEDOM OF ACTION

Experience and the passage of time seem to either make us more tolerant and kindly or to grow critical and calloused to the feelings of others. We probably would deny, even to ourselves, any "hardening of the arteries" of our cordiality toward our fellow human beings.

Habit is an insidious thing, though. Regardless of our perception of skills and intentions, one's personality undergoes constant changes and with those changes, we can win or lose friends without our own conscious knowledge. As a funeral professional, do you ever ask yourself whether the people you contact socially or through the funeral home find it easy to deal with you—easy to like you?

THAT FUNERAL DIRECTOR'S FAMOUS SMILE

This funeral director's character was indefinably, but plainly, part of a superb way in winning friends. Now long gone, he was a courtly, polished gentleman who had a row of gleaming white teeth and a "million-dollar smile." With that smile, his love for humanity exuded from every pore in his body.

It was his spirit that lent real charm to his marvelous ability as a funeral director. He made it easy for people to deal with him and he was at the top of this profession for over 50 years. If his method with people had soured on the way, his career would have been much different.

HE NEVER SITS IN JUDGMENT

A very well-known funeral director from San Diego has a host of friends. A surprising number of people find themselves confiding in him and seeking his advice. The reason for his popularity is that he never sits in judgment upon the other. You'll never hear this man say "I wouldn't have done that" or "You shouldn't have done that"—not even by inference. He never puts another on the defensive. He listens without condemnation and never offers advice unless it is requested. Even then, he makes no recommendation on the basis of "I'll tell you what I think you ought to do." He offers it on the basis of, "Well, my course of procedure would be this," or "What do you think." He still leaves it to his listener to choose his or her own course of action. In short, he is a master in the art of making it easy for the other to talk to and deal with him. In the funeral profession, what we have to sell is a very sensitive and once-in-a-lifetime investment. In our contacts, we must secure goodwill and confidence. In word and manner, we must impose no obligation on the other. That person must be made to feel completely at ease in our presence.

THE CANON OF FUNERAL SERVICE: LET THEM DECIDE FOR THEMSELVES

Most of us like to make up our own minds and form our own decisions without feeling that someone is dominating us, pressing their ideas upon us, or forcing our hand. Nowhere is this more true than in funeral service. Giving information and knowledge to our families, and then letting them feel that they are entirely free from any pressure and acting entirely upon their own judgment makes it easy for them to deal with us, and it authentically invites their confidence and goodwill.

It is a compliment to other people to let them feel that you, as a funeral professional, respect their judgment and their ability to decide. There is a hint of superiority in the attitude that conveys "I want you to do this or that" that makes the object of such a remark or attitude resentful and determined to do nothing at all, if not actually the reverse of what he or she is being pushed to do! Clients and families will usually choose to deal with those who let them exercise their own judgment.

FAMILIES SHY AWAY FROM "PRESSURE"

The funeral director who can gently serve as an organizational specialist and, at the same time, make the families' burdens easier is truly a professional.

To overreach, oversell, overbear, or overattend creates an atmosphere of tension, which can drive families away from us and our funeral homes. Straining to get results is quickly felt by families, and it rarely works. A family can also instantly spot the real thing—a genuine and sincere desire to be of service. The fact that you empower the family to make their own decisions makes it easier for them to deal with you. It is a subtle generosity in itself that frequently causes the family to purchase more from you than they had ever intended.

 DISCUSSION QUESTIONS

1. Do you catch yourself sitting in judgment of others?

2. Do you let people exercise their own judgment? What happens when you don't?

3. Have you ever been complimented for your smile?

4. How does one learn to make people feel more at ease?

37

FAMILIES ARE NOT MIND READERS

"The seeds of knowledge may be planted in solitude, but must be cultivated in public."

Samuel Johnson

 LEARNING OBJECTIVES

- Understand the danger of assuming that people understand more than they do.
- Explain the concept of repackaging the "old stuff."
- Understand the influence of the idea "told them and sold them."
- Explain the importance of giving people the facts.

PEOPLE USUALLY KNOW ONLY WHAT YOU TELL THEM

Some of our greatest difficulties in the funeral service profession in dealing with others arise from the fact that we assume the families' understanding is more complete than it really is.

This is especially true in our profession where terms like niche, church truck, gauge, air-tray, columbarium, trocar, retort, and the like are used. Clearly, the terminology in funeral service is *not* everyday language.

How often do you take for granted that the family knows as much about the funeral home's routine, policies, products, or services as you do?

WORLD'S FAIR STRATEGY

The 1933 Chicago World's Fair was a huge success. In fact, no world's fair since has been that successful.

When the decision was reached to reopen the gates in 1934, a new, gigantic selling task confronted the management. Astute businessmen that they were, they prepared against the public's inclination to regard the fair as "old stuff" and "old-fashioned," nor did they take for granted that the public would know all about the *new* attractions without being told about them.

Thorough promotion in newspapers, magazines, lecture campaigns, and on the radio resold the public on the old attractions and sold the virtues of the new features they would see. People swarmed to the new fair. What turned out to be a glorious success might have been a gigantic flop had the management assumed either that the public would know all about the fair and would attend it again or would somehow know about the new features without being told about them.

This scenario is often seen in funeral homes. The public begins to see the funerals as old stuff or the funeral home as old-fashioned. They drift away to new fads. For this reason, it is very important for the funeral home to creatively repackage the "old stuff" so that it captures the public's attention. For instance, why couldn't a funeral home, instead of advertising air-conditioned chapels and sympathetic service, advertise new caregiving services or profile each staff member?

TO BE FAIR TO YOUR COMMUNITY, TELL THEM!

You see the point. What is old stuff to you is probably an entirely new idea to your families. What your great service will mean to the family cannot possibly be known until *you* tell them.

When you started in funeral service, how many days did you spend in preliminary training, learning how your operation works? Consider, then, a family's helpless lack of understanding as they look to you for answers to their spoken or unspoken questions.

"TOLD THEM AND SOLD THEM"

Many years ago, the Secretary of War in President Hoover's cabinet died suddenly. It was to be a full state military funeral with final burial in the Midwest. When the funeral train and military arrived in the small rural community for the burial, the local funeral director was quickly rebuffed by the high-ranking military.

The funeral director was a close family friend and knew exactly how the funeral should be conducted. He knew his opposition could not be expected to know how much he could really help them unless he told them. Among other things, he explained with infinite patience and clarity that the grave digger would take only opening and closing orders from him and that the cemetery was tricky and he knew how to park cars in the small area. The family wanted him to lower the casket, for it was the deceased's own request. He silenced critics and conducted the funeral.

GIVE FAMILIES THE FACTS

Everyone in funeral service who deals with families must constantly guard against letting their familiarity with funeral merchandise and service options rob their enthusiasm when explaining these vitally important issues to a family.

When you have presented hundreds of caskets, vaults, urns, flowers, and cards, there is a subtle letdown in enthusiasm. It sneaks up on us before we are even aware of it. When we have something new to present, something with interest and appeal, we are enthusiastic about it and we put more energy into our presentation. Families don't know the virtues of the items of service you have until you tell them.

As our merchandise or service becomes an old story to us in the daily routine, we somehow begin to assume that our families also know the details of it—that they are, in other words, mind readers! At that point, we lose untold sales and service opportunities, simply because we do not acquaint families with sufficient information about the thing in question that would enable them to decide wisely and buy.

IMPROVED TELLING EQUALS IMPROVED SELLING

A funeral director decided that she wanted to attract families from the local American Legion and VFW. She made up her mind that she was going to improve her knowledge of military funerals. She began reading all about military funerals, the symbolism of the three volleys, the riderless horse, and the like. In time, she had a library on the subject. Then, she made a small slide program on the symbolism of military funerals and gave the program to all the local American Legion and VFW groups. She never endorsed her own funeral home once.

She was soon getting the bulk of the Legion and VFW services, and her competitor could not compete because he had not told the Legion and VFW so much about military funerals. The Legion and VFW were convinced that only the lady funeral director who had so much to talk about could yield the service results they wanted.

YOUR RESPONSIBILITY

As a professional, you cannot expect your families to ask all the questions that will give them the necessary facts upon which they make a decision. The responsibility of answering unspoken questions and supplying the confidence is yours. Although they may not always show it, families appreciate it when a funeral director is interested enough in them to give them a thorough understanding of products or services.

The only assumption you can safely make is that your families know only as much or as little about what you have to sell as you tell. Telling the facts of this great profession in an interesting way attracts families to you and contributes to your success in every way!

DISCUSSION QUESTIONS

1. How can we be sure to cover all the information our families need?

2. What are some ways to creatively repackage funeral service to make the "old stuff" seem new? Decide on one new idea.

3. In pairs, practice telling the benefits of at least two items of funeral service (role play).

4. In what areas do you feel that you need to expand on your telling skills?

38

THROUGH THE FAMILIES' EYES

"The greater man, the greater courtesy."

Alfred Lord Tennyson

 LEARNING OBJECTIVES

- Understand the idea that families are self-centered.

- Understand and appreciate the Frank E. Campbell quote.

- Be able to explain the differences between self-centered service vs. unexpected service and unselfish service.

- Explain the lesson of the trapped miners story.

SERVE THE FAMILIES' SELFISH INTEREST

The characteristics of selfishness are never pleasing. Watch people who are gambling. They generally indicate by the gleaming eyes, flushed cheeks, and tense nerves that they are blind to anyone's interest other than their own.

It is easy to detect selfishness and self-interest in someone else, but as funeral professionals, we should never forget that others are weighing us by the same yardstick. In moments of reflection, we know that to win a friend, we must see through the other person's eyes and accommodate our actions to meet that family's or individual's desires.

In our profession, we must bear in mind that the clients/families are the most important people in the world. If you are receiving a family, it will often surprise you how quickly you can obtain their goodwill by concentrating on *their* interests.

STAND MENTALLY ALONGSIDE THE FAMILY

One of the most famous funeral directors in the history of our great profession, Frank E. Campbell of New York City, once made this observation:

> To me the most successful service to a family is only achieved when we put ourselves in their shoes. If we can learn to stand mentally alongside the family—seeing through their eyes—sensing their attitude toward ourselves and what we are doing and selling, we more rapidly fall in step with their thoughts and hence the funeral becomes an experience of value.

Campbell wrote this in 1919, and the lesson is just as valuable to us today as it was those many years ago.

SELF-CENTERED SERVICE LOSES CONFIDENCE

There are far too many of us in funeral service who seem to never get away from *our* side of expectations. We seem to never get into the families' shoes. We might get the call, make a sale, and do a funeral, but do we make the service as valuable, meaningful, or creative as it can be?

Serving the clients from their side of the equation results in more helpful service, and that is what all families are ultimately looking for. They appreciate it, but in reality, it is something they seldom get anywhere.

Acquiring the ability to see through the other person's eyes is something none of us can achieve overnight. This attitude toward service (in our profession anyway) is learned by any individual only through personal observation, study, and practice.

All products and services offer distinct uses or advantages. The suppliers in our profession have done an outstanding job in creativity and innovation. It is up to us to *individualize* them to our families—show how the offerings of merchandise will make their tasks of mourning easier, contribute to their peace of mind, and make their adjustments to life more productive.

Our attitude of service always must be one of "This is to *your* (the families') advantage. The quality is for *your* benefit. You will find peace of mind with *this* feature. We have done this service because it accomplishes *this* for you," and so on.

UNEXPECTED SERVICE: THE TRAVEL GUIDE

Going beyond the routine of giving service is not particularly difficult and it need not be expensive.

A prime example of this came to me in my travels several years ago. I visited a funeral home in Calgary, Alberta, Canada, and had a delightful conversation with the receptionist. I asked her about her job and her life and then asked her how she performed her role of answering the door in the same way night after night without getting bored.

She very innocently told me her procedure, and I thought it was wonderful. She had gone to the bookstore and had purchased travel guides about all places in the United States and the Dominion of Canada. When she would arrive at work, she would read the vital statistics and get the locations of all the relatives. Then, before the family came to the visitation, she would read up on the various towns and cities where the family members came from. When the family came in, she would introduce herself and ask "Where do you live?" The reply would be "Detroit" or some other place. The receptionist would then begin to share what she had read about Detroit and the people were delighted. It made them feel comfortable, it gave her something to talk about, and it made for a solid relationship between her and the family.

"GET THEM OUT OF HERE TODAY!"

Many years ago, two men were entombed in a gold mine at Moose River, Nova Scotia. For 10 days in cramped, chilly quarters, on a narrow shelf just above icy water that was waist deep, Dr. D. E. Robertson and Alfred Scalding awaited the heroic efforts of hardy mine workers to rescue them. Hugh McPherson of Stellarton, one of the rescue workers, climbed off a sick bed to work day and night to dig down to the imprisoned men. He and his fellows pictured to themselves the predicament of the victims and dug like madmen. "I'm going to stay here until I get those poor devils out of there," was the attitude of McPherson that characterized the heroism that finally rescued the trapped men.

THE LESSON

Down under the surface of outward appearances are families who need our help. They are in a mighty big predicament because of death and grief, and are without the benefit of what the funeral profession has to offer. Let's get their viewpoint and *serve* them!

HOW WE DO THINGS

It's all in attitude—are we going to be service driven, or self-service driven? Here are a couple of examples of service versus self-service. You be the judge.

A man wanted to trade in his old car. One car salesman said, "Sure is an old one, isn't it?" and appraised it at $1,000.

The next salesman said, "It looks as though you have really taken care of it and that the car has been given mighty fine service." He, too, appraised it at $1,000. He closed the sale. He had the right attitude. He brought his client's interest into the picture.

I was once shopping at the old Shillito Department Store in Cincinnati and observed this example of service versus self-service. It was raining outside. I noticed that as customers were entering the store, only one of the many sales clerks was helping people with their raincoats and umbrellas. This salesperson even offered to keep watch on their rain gear until their shopping was finished. What was amazing to me was that the greatest number of people, when they returned to her for their raincoats, actually made purchases from this salesperson! Once more, serving the customer's self-interest made the difference.

The story is told of a manager of a jewelry store who happened to serve a man interested in buying a fountain pen. After a brief size-up of his customer, the manager brought out a tray of $15 pens. The customer smiled at this and gently kidded, "Don't you think that is a little too rich for my blood?" The manager's comeback was swift and expert, "Not at all, sir. In fact, I was reaching for a tray of higher-priced pens, but somebody had evidently switched them." He then put the $15 tray back and produced one with pens ranging much higher.

The customer selected an $80 pen. The point is that the salesman jumped into the customer's shoes the instant the customer made his kidding remarks. He sensed immediately, of course, that here was a man able and willing to buy because people, as a rule, who do not have as much ready money will throw out an economy hint rather than joke about price.

UNSELFISH SERVICE

In unselfish service, you submerge your own personality to the families. Far from being self-centered, you are the master of service given willingly. You are making an easier time of it for all parties when you adopt this service attitude. You are making a friend for yourself and for your funeral home.

Never forget that the funeral service world still holds out its richest rewards to people who possess the faculty of attracting clients/families.

DISCUSSION QUESTIONS

1. Share your experiences of times when you have stood empathetically alongside the family.

2. Discuss examples of how self-centered service loses confidence.

3. Do you think the travel guide concept is a good idea? If not, can you offer other ideas?

4. Offer examples and discuss your own experiences with service versus self-service.

39

PUT YOURSELF IN THE OTHER PERSON'S SHOES

"It is not the shilling I give you that counts, but the warmth that it carries with it from my hand."

Miguel de Unamuno

LEARNING OBJECTIVES

- Understand how to look for clues in viewing the family.
- Demonstrate how we learn preferences by letting people talk.
- Appreciate how important it is to get the viewpoint of the family.
- Explain the concept of cooperatively generating ideas.

One of the most vital considerations in winning the friendship and cooperation of others, particularly the families we serve and the people with whom we work, is the ability to *understand* them.

Each person is truly a world unto him- or herself. Everyone has individual viewpoints, individual faults, and individual likes and dislikes. If we were all living independent, selfish lives that did not require us to serve our families or to associate with others, we would not have to make any effort whatsoever to understand them.

However, those who choose funeral service as a career face the necessity of understanding others—of making people feel that we see their problems and their point of view. Thus, you often gain information of value to yourself and to your funeral home and a better understanding of human nature that proves useful in many ways.

LOOK FOR CLUES

Watch for indications of a family's preferences. You will often be enabled to render distinctive service that will exceed their expectations and will establish loyalty to your funeral home.

Probably the greatest clue in dealing with a family is to look into their feelings concerning grief. It is a rare situation that grief is absent when a death occurs, and one of the best ways to get into the soul of the bereaved is to recall how painful it was when you lost someone or something of great significance.

LEARN THEIR PREFERENCES BY LETTING THEM TALK

A highly successful funeral director in Chicago was well versed in dealing with others' viewpoints. His strategy was to ask open-ended questions and just let them talk. He always opened the arrangement conference with these two questions: "What was the last funeral you attended?" and "What did you find helpful in that experience?"

The object of his questions in this exact order was to find out the family's preferences—their likes and dislikes. Throughout the conference, he would carefully note the family's comments and hence was able to design a funeral versus arrange one.

Study the other person's reasoning. Try to learn his or her preferences and point of view. It will help you deal with others in a tactful, understanding way that will invite their confidence and goodwill. Remember, not everyone is so thoughtful! Families will then seek you out to your own advantage.

GETTING VIEWPOINTS WINS FAMILIES

A Phoenix funeral director was making arrangements for the funeral of an elderly woman who was survived by one daughter. The funeral director's procedures in the selection room were totally indirect. In other words, he never went into the selection room. He explained all the caskets in the arrangement room and opened the door to the selection room and let the daughter in. One hour later, she had not returned and the funeral director went into the room. The woman stood there frozen and said she could not select any casket.

The funeral director calmly asked her what she thought was holding her back. She said she was scared to death to be in the room by herself. The funeral director abandoned his mindset of the "indirect" approach and went in with her to make the selection.

Had an effort not been made to learn this woman's objection, she might have been antagonized, which would have resulted in a lose–lose situation.

Let us never judge hastily! Always try to understand the other person's side. Often, a costly quarrel can develop when we refuse to consider the other person's viewpoint.

GIVING CREDIT FOR IDEAS WINS COOPERATION

A pre-need manager in a large cemetery habitually brought new ideas to managerial conferences. His ideas were often complimented and adopted. However, he was palming off the ideas of his subordinates as his own. The people in the pre-need department learned of it, and an undercurrent of bad feelings developed. Finally, rumblings reached the owner of the cemetery. He endeavored to gain the viewpoint of the employees. Succeeding in this, he took disciplinary action with the offending executive. Had that individual acknowledged the authorship of the ideas he received and unselfishly credited his associates, they would have worked harder than ever to cooperate with him, and his own fairness and bigness of character would have been established in the minds of all.

Endeavor to gain the other person's point of view, but only with the idea of cooperating with him or her to the advantage of all. Be open minded and considerate of the circumstances that cause the other person to think as he or she does. Such consideration pays *you* dividends in increased efficiency, friendships, business, and opportunity for advancement.

 DISCUSSION QUESTIONS

1. Give examples of how important it is for people to understand you.

2. Give examples of clues you give out in order to be understood.

3. List the values of getting the family's viewpoint.

4. How have you responded when someone has taken credit for your idea?

40

THE TIMID FAMILY

"Kindness is the golden chain by which society is bound together."
Johann Wolfgang von Goethe

LEARNING OBJECTIVES

- Develop a respectful and sensitive attitude toward timid families.

- Understand the value of gentleness in the funeral profession.

- Develop the ability to not judge people by appearances.

- Respect the value of a cautious attitude in funeral service.

PUT FAMILIES AT EASE

Several years ago, a study analyzing customers was performed. The conclusion of this study was the amazing fact that 78 percent of the public are "timid." Timid! And you thought people were so bold.

The fact is that most people are timid and persuadable. The reason we all think we meet so many bold people is the exaggerated impression they leave on us.

If 78 out of every 100 people we contact in the funeral home are not sure of themselves—bashful or ill at ease—we must be constantly on guard not to upset, rush, or push and then drive away many of the loyalties of this large percentage of the population.

SHE ACTS SHY HERSELF

A highly successful receptionist in a funeral home in Minneapolis has a clever way of handling the timid person. She says: "A bustling, officious receptionist in a funeral home can scare a shy person. So I act as if I am of shy temperament myself, with quiet understanding to respect their feelings and wishes. Many people are uncomfortable. I put them at ease by telling them I will be glad to help them in any way that they wish. That is what I am here for."

THINGS THAT PEOPLE DISLIKE

A man came into a funeral home once to request additional copies of a death certificate. The man whispered his wish to the receptionist who was sitting at the desk. As the receptionist rose, she saw the funeral home manager and said quite loudly, "Mr. Jones needs some more death certificates for his nephew. Wasn't he the boy who took his own life?"

Many people have blushed to their hair roots because some softly spoken request was relayed in bellowing tones by another person who knew little about human nature and not enough about his or her profession.

WHEN YOU WIN THEM, YOU KEEP THEM

Because so many people are bashful and timid, particularly around a funeral home, careful handling of these people is truly a wise course to follow. They will associate with your funeral home by being cautious and unwilling to take a chance on dealing elsewhere.

A normal tone of voice, coupled with an encouraging smile, will put most timid people at ease. They sense that you understand, and understanding is paramount in our profession.

APPEARANCE IS NO GAUGE OF BUYING POWER

A man whose sister had just died at a local hospital came into the funeral home. As the funeral director came to help the man, he could not help but notice that the man was poorly dressed. He was clean, but his clothes were very plain and simple.

The bereaved man explained that he and his family had moved from the Orient to the United States years before and that he and his sister had operated a small food store for many years. The man also explained that his wife had died before the move to the States and that he still had her cremated remains at home.

The funeral director paid no attention to this man's appearance. He spent a lot of time with the old man and gave him every option of services and products available. In the end, the gentleman purchased not only a significant cremation service but a new urn for his first wife.

This is a concrete example of proper handling. The general rule should be to treat all families with the same care and consideration that timid families must be accorded if their confidence is to be won. Put them all at their ease. Assume, no matter what their outward demeanor, that they are "timid customers" who want to feel free to make their own decisions as much as they want their business to be regarded as confidential.

DISCUSSION QUESTIONS

1. Give examples of timid people you know and how you treat them.

2. Share experiences of times when you have been timid. What helped you the most?

3. Make a list of irritating habits that you dislike.

4. Offer examples of when you judged someone by his or her appearance. What was the outcome?

41

ADVICE

"When a man seeks your advice he generally wants your praise."
Philip Dormer Stanhope Chesterfield

 LEARNING OBJECTIVES

- Understand the concept of the dangers of giving too much advice.
- Explain the idea of the community selection room.
- Be able to explain the dangers of giving too little advice.
- Define the term *suggestion*.

"I DON'T NEED YOUR ADVICE"

These words have been spoken many times or thought in resentment against someone else who, with a know-it-all attitude, tried to force their suggestions and opinions on others.

Families and clients resent this attitude because, in reality, we are all individuals. Most of us want to live our own lives, do our own thinking, and enjoy complete freedom of action. If we want advice or suggestions, we ask for it and so do our families.

How to go about making suggestions to our families without offending the other person's sense of individuality, therefore, is an outstanding factor in successfully dealing with others. A sincere desire to serve families may cause us to be just a little too eager to please. Advice or suggestions offered with insistent repetition may secretly annoy a family and cause them to feel pressured.

THE COMMUNITY SELECTION ROOM

A very innovative and creative funeral director in Portland, Maine, created a selection room that required just the right amount of advice when caskets were shown. Because this funeral director believed that families overlooked and/or did not listen to lengthy explanations, he devised the community casket room concept. He sent casket photos to several hundred randomly chosen people and asked each person to select a casket that he or she liked. He then compiled all the results, and those were the caskets he put on his floor—not the caskets *he* liked, but the caskets *they* liked. Then, he could truly say, "These caskets represent the type and style that this community prefers." He discovered, to his delight, that the advice he gave about caskets was enhanced tenfold by his insight and consideration to not give too much advice, too fast, in too short a time span.

HOW YOU ADVISE IS IMPORTANT

You can gain quiet enjoyment by noting the ego of others that is often expressed in the solemn wagging of a finger with the phrase, "You mark my words." Human nature likes to predict, make prophecies, and offer advice. When we realize how much the average family values their own opinion and judgment, it is plain that any suggestions we may hope to offer successfully must be offered with modesty, humility, and diplomacy. This is what that creative funeral director accomplished with the community selection room.

We will be happier and get along better, particularly when dealing with families, by adopting the "humility of the truly great." Nathaniel Hawthorne, the famous author, had a modest, philosophical attitude toward his work that saved him from stress and strain and made him popular and pleasing to deal with. Hawthorne said it was a great honor to be a man of letters, although he always knew that most of what was printed of his own writings "will be used to light a fire, or, if read at all, to gather dirt on a shelf."

Naturally, you want to serve your families and have them continue to use your funeral home. We may even be authorities in this profession, but remember, "advice" given at the wrong time or in the wrong way, is seldom appreciated. Use the art of the suggestion. Families must feel that they are voluntarily making decisions. Present the facts concerning their funeral options, and let them decide their own course of action. If the family asks for your advice, that is a different matter. Offer it modestly, though; don't push it on them.

THE SUGGESTION

Making an invisible or indirect suggestion rarely makes a family "rile up," because you are planting the seeds of ideas they probably have never thought about. I once knew a highly successful pre-need insurance representative from New York City. In discussing a policy, she would always say, "I think the smartest thing *we* can do is to go over this agreement together, don't you?" After reading the policy, she would sit back and say, "Well, what do *you* think of it, Mr. Grey? Does that seem to cover the type of protection you want, or should we see what this other company has to offer?"

Funeral service today requires a "partnership affair." You cannot have the attitude of Big Me telling Little You what you ought to have.

It is only common courtesy to all the families to experience "free choice" in arriving at their decisions. By keeping your suggestions "invisible," you help to influence their decision and at the same time run minimal risk of having the family turn on you with the words or thought of "I don't need your advice."

DISCUSSION QUESTIONS

1. Give examples of how you like to receive advice.

2. How does advice rub you the wrong way?

3. Discuss the ideal way to offer advice.

4. Practice giving each other suggestions concerning funeral options.

VI

FUNERAL SERVICE ETIQUETTE

"Manners are of more importance than laws. Upon them in a great measure, the laws depend. The law touches us but here and there, and now and then. Manners are what vex or soothe, corrupt or purify, exalt or debase, barbarize or refine us, by a constant, steady, uniform, insensible operation, like that of the air we breathe."

Edmund Burke

42

THE POWER OF "THANK YOU"

"Kind words cost no more than unkind ones, . . . and we may
scatter the seeds of courtesy and kindliness around us at so little
expense. If you would fall into any extreme, let it be on the side of
gentleness. The human mind is so constructed that it resists vigor
and yields to softness."
Jeremy Bentham

LEARNING OBJECTIVES

- Understand the concept that families always deserve recognition.
- Explain the power behind a "thank you."
- Understand and elaborate on the theme that funeral service is a matter of the heart.
- Understand the domino effect of courtesy.

CLIENTS ALWAYS DESERVE RECOGNITION

The old man's wife was dead. He came to the funeral home to make arrangements. The funeral director took the information, the man selected funeral products, and everything seemed set. But something was missing—something was wrong.

The old man got up from his chair, the funeral director nodded a type of "good-bye," and that was it! The old man had just invested $4,000 for his wife's funeral and he received a nod.

As the old man left the funeral home, he couldn't stand it any longer. He looked square in the funeral director's face and

said, "Young man, you need to learn the value of saying thank you! There are numerous other funeral homes I could have selected, but I came here. Maybe I'm funny, but you could have thanked me for selecting your firm. Would that be asking too much?"

The funeral director was stunned. He had never thought to thank a client for selecting his funeral home, but he knew the old man was right.

A "THANK YOU" IS ALWAYS APPRECIATED

We can all sympathize with the feelings of the old man. We have all been occasionally stung by someone's failure to say "thank you." Those two words are vitally important—especially in funeral service!

Upon concluding the arrangements, the funeral director might have said, "We are here to help you and thank you for the trust you have placed in our firm." This short phrase would have made all the difference in the world. Why? Because human nature is extremely sensitive. We all crave appreciation and recognition.

A MATTER OF HEART

To register favorably, a "thank you" must come from the heart; it must be a convincing impression of gratitude and appreciation. A weak, mechanical "thank you" is almost worse than none at all. The simple fact that bereaved clients keep the funeral home in operation should make it natural for us to think kindly of them and thank them with unmistakable appreciation for their confidence, trust, and patronage. The truth is that they could easily have gone somewhere else.

No one benefits more from consistent and authentic courtesy than one who practices it. Which personality wins friends and favorable recognition—the kindly, appreciative person or the attitude that suggests "the world owes me a living and if you don't like what I do, you can leave, quit, go somewhere else, or jump in the lake?" Professional arrogance of this type is not only dangerous but has absolutely no purpose in the funeral service profession.

FUNERAL DIRECTOR'S COURTESY: THE DOMINO EFFECT

Every sincere "thank you" and act of courtesy has a domino effect, a long-arm effect. We can never fully realize what tremendous benefits we gain for ourselves and our firms when we make thoughtfulness and thankfulness a daily habit.

A funeral director from Indiana conducted a funeral one hot summer afternoon in a church that had no air conditioning. The funeral was long and the soloist was scheduled to sing three hymns. By the time the funeral started, the mercury was right at 100 degrees. The soloist sang her first hymn. When she finished the second, it became clear that she was truly uncomfortable.

The funeral director, seeing this situation from the back of the church, went downstairs, filled a large glass with ice and wa-

ter, and took it to the front of the church. As he handed the refreshment to the drained soloist, he whispered, "This is a thank
you for your beautiful music today."

The soloist's family had always used another funeral
home, but when the soloist's mother died some years later, this
funeral director was called to serve. His "thank you" had won a
new client.

PRESIDENT LINCOLN'S HONEST COURTESY

Lincoln had an unusual campaign practice. He would ask vot-
ers directly whether or not they intended to vote for him. If
they said "No," Lincoln would smile good naturedly and ask,
"Why not?" Then, he would try to clear up any problem or
questions in the voter's mind. Upon leaving, Lincoln would say,
"Thank you for your time, and I hope for your vote!"

If the voter said, "Yes," Lincoln would cordially shake the
person's hand, and say, "Thank you. It's always good to know
who your friends are." If a voter still frankly declared it his intention not to vote for Lincoln, the long-legged lawyer would
smilingly say, "Well, thank you for being frank. We're still good
friends just the same." Lincoln once explained his strategy:
"The questions give me a chance to say 'thank you' to my enemies, and I have found I gain more friends the more I say
'Thank you.' "

"Thank you" smooths the way in human relations in the
funeral service profession, but the words must be accompanied
by the "music!"

DISCUSSION QUESTIONS

1. Do you always remember to thank people?

2. Do you remember to especially thank difficult families?

3. How do you define the domino effect? List examples.

4. What will help you remember to thank families?

43

OLD-FASHIONED MANNERS

"Manners cost nothing, and buys everything."
Lady Mary Wortley Montague

 LEARNING OBJECTIVES

- Understand the basics in the process of winning a following.
- Be able to explain why the client has the right to every possible consideration.
- Explain how courtesy week works.
- Understand the danger of indifference in funeral service.

ONE SURE WAY TO WIN A FOLLOWING

The owner of one of the largest funeral homes in the world relays this story: He once made a surprise visit to one of his own branch locations. During the visit, he overheard a client complaining to the funeral home attendant about the quality of service. Questioned later by the owner, the attendant explained that the man was an ill-mannered crank and that no one could please him. "Of course he is," replied the proprietor, "but it is *our* business to please cranks. Anyone can please a gentleman."

Every day we come in contact with people of all types, many of whom are hard to please and ill mannered, who judge us by what we say and do. We all know too that a bad-tempered individual is avoided, even though his appearance may be pleasing. Conversely, some plain person may win the hearts of everyone merely by the charm of his manners.

A following for either a person or a funeral home is not accomplished by any feats of "rabbit-out-of-the-hat" magic.

Clients are won through time-honored good service, attentiveness, courtesy, and kindness.

TO ATTRACT OTHERS, BE CONSIDERATE!

Observing the rules of good conduct, that is, being courteous, thoughtful, and patient, is as essential in a profession as it is socially. You really cannot separate the three. Nearly every successful funeral home can trace its success to the thoughtful service of the men and women who work there.

Good manners are the art of doing the correct thing at the right time and showing consideration for the other person. Simple, isn't it? With such a creed, countless men and women in funeral service have climbed from the rut of day-to-day routine to heights of leadership in this profession. People without this creed may appear successful, but, in reality, they have failed at a key component of life.

This key component, this truth about funeral manners is this: *The client has a right to every possible consideration!* If we adopt this as a rule, we are positioned to maximize our efforts to make friends.

WINNING AN IMPATIENT CLIENT

A top-notch funeral director ignores the sharp tongues and hasty actions of ill-mannered clients and always focuses on finding solutions to the problems that have created their nasty looks and sour remarks.

A funeral director in Michigan relays this story: "Recently, I was standing in the foyer of the funeral home. Suddenly, a woman rushed up to me and said, 'I have never seen such a place as this. I want some more acknowledgement cards and I can't get anyone to wait on me!' It was right in the middle of my conversation with another family. I apologized and quickly decided I would have to do something special, something beyond just getting her a box of cards, to soothe her. I was determined not only to please her momentarily and to soothe her, but to ensure her goodwill and future patronage.

I followed up on my apology by showering her with extra attention. I had her taken to my private office. We relieved her of the bundles she had been carrying and brought her a hot cup of tea and a Danish. Then I sat down with her, talked to her for 10 minutes, and asked if she needed a ride home. She said yes, and I instructed one of our people to pull the sedan around to the front door of the funeral home. The last thing I did was get her the box of cards. She was all smiles as she left, and I received a thank-you note from her a week later."

ADOPTED COURTESY WEEK

Good manners are so essential in the funeral service profession that a suggestion that every manager of every funeral home should consider is to have a *courtesy week.*

The courtesy week concept involves the members of the funeral home staff keeping a log of every courteous act that they perform in a week's time. At the end of the week, everyone compares notes and each learns additional methods of courtesy from one another.

It is a powerful concept. When we cultivate good people from top to bottom on a consistent basis, people are attracted to us and we will enjoy the satisfaction that comes from an ever-growing personal following. Have you ever wondered why some funeral directors have a following and some don't? Much of the success of a following can be linked to courtesy.

Clients, particularly funeral clients, are extremely sensitive to any lack of consideration. They are hurt and resentful when they do not receive individual attention and respect from funeral practitioners—and rightfully so!

INDIFFERENCE: THE CANCER IN SOCIETY

An example of this type of malignancy in funeral service is the "I'm just doing you a favor by waiting on you" attitude. This always is a dead-end street for a funeral director.

A funeral director ran into an interesting situation several years ago when confronted with a family that was personally visiting funeral homes and comparing prices. When the family came into the funeral home, they were candid about their mission. The funeral director took them into the office and gave them a general price list and said he had to leave for a minute. He went to the employee lounge and gossiped for a few minutes with the other employees. A minute turned into five, five minutes into ten, and after fifteen minutes, when the funeral director returned to the office, the family was gone.

That afternoon, the manager of the funeral home heard about the incident and the people involved. He cornered the offending funeral director. "What on earth is the matter with you, Jim?" "Oh," said Jim, "they were just a bunch of shoppers. They weren't going to buy anything from us, anyway." "Shoppers," the manager thundered, "why, those people have used our funeral home for years. You fumbled this terribly. You should have flooded them with attention!"

That fumbling funeral director was also a "shopper" the next day—for a job!

WE GO WHERE WE ARE WELCOME

To be indifferent or condescending, to be curt with clients, or to indicate by manner or tone of voice that we think they are too hard to please are bad manners and have no place in our noble profession.

To be helpful, pleasant, patient, accommodating, and considerate in our contacts with clients and associates are the cornerstones of funeral service that enable us to build enduring relationships and our own professional future by building up the great funeral home that we represent.

DISCUSSION QUESTIONS

1. How can you win over an impatient family?

2. Why are manners so important?

3. How would you implement a courtesy week?

4. Give some examples of how you have gone beyond the call of duty. What happened as a result?

44

THE IMPRESSION YOU GIVE

"If you would stand well with a great mind, leave him with a favorable impression of yourself; if with a little mind, leave him with a favorable opinion of himself."

Samuel Taylor Coleridge

 LEARNING OBJECTIVES

- Identify where friendliness and smiles start.

- Understand why it is vital to make a good impression.

- Understand how impression building is so economical for the funeral home.

- Explain why funeral service is in a fish bowl.

WHICH IMPRESSION DO YOU CREATE?

Whether we know it or not, the most candid of all cameras—the observation, reaction, and impression of everyone we contact—is constantly focused on us. No profession is in a fish bowl more than funeral service.

The "picture" others get of you in the funeral home is important because it either goes into their album of "People I Like to Deal With" or joins the miscellaneous file of "People Who Are a Pain in the Neck."

What people see in your face is important. Your face expresses friendliness or its opposite; it is a reflection of your thoughts. If you present a stoic, indifferent front, the inference is that you do not mentally value the individual with the "camera." In our profession, that person may be the means of helping or profoundly hindering your career and success. If a funeral professional lands in the album of "People Who Are a Pain in the Neck," it means loss for you and possible catastrophe for the mortuary.

Did you ever notice the warm, friendly smiles you get from a salesperson at a five-star store or restaurant? Did you ever see them looking grouchy? Not many! A smile and a warm handshake are at the top of the list of essential attributes of all five-star personalities. Most successful managers know that they get more money, attention, and respect for being friendly than from just the "stuff" they perform daily. Hanging a coat in a funeral home isn't worth a penny, but the friendly smile that accompanies the courteous gesture is the frosting on the cake.

We all should feel free to express a smile, even to grieving people. A smile can take on all sorts of meaning. A sympathetic smile is indeed a genuine comfort to our families. Study the effect on your associates when you express your warm heart to others and you will wonder why you haven't smiled more and why other people don't smile more!

A cheerless, mentally indifferent attitude in contacts with families can drive away business. In fact, sometimes business failures can be traced to smile and friendliness failure!

WHERE IT STARTS

Friendliness and smiles always start in the mind, and because mental attitudes either make us or break us, it can truly be said that our success with people in part lurks at the corners of one's mouth!

When you think well of people and visualize their problems, their rights, their good intentions, what the possibility of their cooperation holds for you, and what your considerate treatment means to them, you just naturally reflect that understanding in your face. It is a real plus for any funeral professional to be able to do this.

Eleanor Roosevelt once said, "Smiles and friendliness furnish the light and warmth for the world which otherwise would be stark and cold."

FRIENDLY APPRECIATION

Families, and no one else, make it possible for us to have our jobs and for our funeral homes and cemeteries to prosper.

Then, why shouldn't they receive a smile and friendly appreciation? When a funeral home is lighted and warmed with friendly
people, the formula for success is also present. People feel better about calling and dealing with such an organization.

Several years ago, a funeral director shared this story of a
conversation he overheard between two men at a visitation.
The two men were chatting in the lobby of the funeral home.
In discussing their reactions to the service encountered at various funeral homes, one said, "I like this funeral home, although my family has usually called Fred down the street. The
people here make you feel welcome, give you a friendly smile
and greeting, and cheerfully go out of their way to serve you.
It's not pretentious, but it's homey—it's human. I prefer it here
to the place down the street; they are indifferent and cold."
The other man heartily agreed.

Your fellow workers, your funeral home's families, everyone reacts the same way to friendliness. Smiles and warm hand-
shakes are such inexpensive goodwill builders—yet how miserly
we spend them!

IT TAMED A GROUCH

It is true that a smile is the most disarming weapon in the
world. One day, a young man who wanted to become a funeral
director approached a funeral director in his town about the
possibility of learning something about funeral service. The
older funeral director was an old grouch who glared and
snorted at the young man, "You—a funeral director? Why,
you're nothing but a fool!" The young man, ignoring the blus-
tering, smiled from ear to ear. "Why, sir," he said, "I only want
to be like you when I grow up. Tell you what, I'll work for you
for nothing for a month and then you can decide if I'm a fool
or not."

The old funeral director took him up on his offer and a
month later put the young man to work full time. It was the
friendly attitude of the young man that won over the old
grouchy funeral director.

Not everyone can cash in on a friendly attitude so quickly
or directly, but it pays dividends in satisfaction just to see a person's face light up in response.

Some readers will quickly remember the late Bert Parks,
who for years was the master of ceremonies for the Miss America contest. He was once asked why most contestants were eventually eliminated and rejected. "That's easy," he replied, "no

matter how beautifully you dress a show window, it's no good until you turn on the lights." He was referring to that great attitude of a warm, irresistible, dazzling, warm, sunny impression that the winner always possesses.

That's the truth in a nutshell. Friendly impressions light up people, revealing the real essence of a person's character. With friendliness and smiles, you surround yourself and your funeral home, and the world in which you move, with that "light and warmth" so desirable in all funeral service endeavors.

Eleanor Roosevelt once said, "After my husband died, I had two choices: either curse the darkness or light candles so I could see. I chose the latter, and it has made all the difference in the world."

DISCUSSION QUESTIONS

1. Describe people you have met who are "a pain in the neck."

2. Why do you think it is hard for some people to smile?

3. Can you smile too much in a funeral home?

4. Discuss how you would "tame a grouch."

45

OVERFAMILIARITY BREEDS RESENTMENT

"Let us teach ourselves that honorable step, not to outdo discretion."

William Shakespeare

LEARNING OBJECTIVES

- Appreciate and respect the danger point of familiarity.

- Understand the concept that everyone is important in funeral service.

- Understand what Churchill meant by "too much tongue."

- Explain and elaborate on being reserved in funeral service.

THERE IS A DANGER POINT

We all know the advantages an attitude of friendliness creates. A constant friendliness and willingness to cooperate brings employees and families of our funeral homes close to us. In many ways that we may never hear about, they boost and serve us.

However, there is a point where friendliness ends and dangerous familiarity begins. Even the wisest of us sometimes forget this, always to our regret.

Take newcomers in the funeral home. For the first few days or weeks they "walk softly" to make a good impression. They gradually become acquainted with their fellow workers. If they take this attitude of friendliness for familiarity, they are making a mistake.

More than likely, the very ones they familiarly question or try to "kid" don't like being asked personal questions or being kidded by anyone, least of all by an inquisitive newcomer. Resentment quickly grows until everyone regards the newcomer as a pest and takes every occasion to help this person "out" of the funeral home.

THE VETERAN FUNERAL DIRECTOR'S RESPECT

I once worked for a great American funeral director, Cornelius P. Heafey, who had received his license in 1919. He was devoutly committed to the "old school" in funeral service. He had steel rules about conduct at a funeral. One rule was that no matter what happened at a funeral, no matter what tension or crisis, no matter who the funeral was for, and no matter where the funeral was held, all the men working at the funeral were required to address each other as "Mister." My mentor was convinced that the only way his staff could endure working so close together in such stressful situations and keep respect for one another at a service was to hold each other off at arm's length with "Mister." It sounds old-fashioned today, but it did help keep us on our toes yesterday.

EVERYONE IS IMPORTANT

In funeral service, the wise man or woman treats all associates with respect. Regardless of another's station in life, you cannot go wrong by treating that person with consideration and courtesy.

As important as it is not to overstep the line of respect in the inner circles of the funeral home, it is even more important in our attitude toward families. Therein, familiarity breeds resentment that results in lost business, lost profits, and lost opportunities.

CUSTOMERS ARE PROUD

When I was a young man, I saw this happen. My aunt operated a grocery store in our town and had one assistant. A large, stout man with a pleasant disposition had recently moved to our town. One day, I was in the grocery store at the same time as this newcomer. I started to visit with him while standing in line, waiting to be checked out. As I approached the checkout, my aunt's young assistant looked at me and said in a tone loud enough to be heard by this large man, "Who's your fat friend?" I froze, my aunt almost fainted, and my new friend, who had selected a big basket of groceries, stalked out without a word. My aunt rightfully fired her assistant on the spot.

ALERT! No words can tell how wrong that clerk was, nor how wrong any person contacting the public is who mistakes decent friendliness on the part of the client as a "go-signal" for making personal remarks!!!

NO ONE SHOULD BE TAKEN FOR GRANTED

General Douglas MacArthur, one of our nation's outstanding military leaders, habitually traded at a little shop in the seaside town where he summered. Although peppery in disposition, the old General always seemed to enjoy a few words with the proprietor. One afternoon, General MacArthur came in and was about to make a purchase when a wild-haired "summer resorter" dashed to the counter.

The proprietor proceeded to serve her, although General MacArthur was undeniably there first. The General's face clouded. He turned and walked stiffly toward the door. "Oh, General MacArthur," called the storekeeper, "just a second now—surely an old customer like you doesn't mind my waiting on this lady first." MacArthur turned and roared, "I mind it extremely, sir. I shall never darken this door again."

Why should that store owner have thought he could take MacArthur's patronage for granted? Why should any of us take for granted *any* customer's patronage merely because he or she is friendly or has used our funeral home for a long time?

THE BARBER'S MISTAKE

The funeral director who gave me my first job had used a certain barber for years. One day, my boss came back to the office from the barber shop, raging like a lion. The all-perfect barber had presumed on my boss's good nature and loyalty by asking him for a loan. I remember my boss's response. "I couldn't very well refuse him, but it made me boil to think he would make a mark out of me just because I had been a good customer. I'll never go there again!"

That is an extreme example of overfamiliarity. In many instances, friends and customers are being driven away by people who do not seem to know where friendliness ends and poisonous familiarity begins.

TALKED HIMSELF OUT OF CUSTOMERS

A Chicago funeral director told me this story: The funeral director had been having all the cars from the business serviced by a certain service station for three years. As time went by, he became increasingly annoyed by the overtalkativeness of the young proprietor, who began to kid him familiarly and talk at length about funeral home matters and of particular unnatural death calls the funeral home had handled. Worse, he would keep talking even when this funeral director showed unmistakably that he was in a hurry to be off. The result was that this funeral director pulled all his business from the service station.

TOO MUCH!

Winston Churchill was a loyal customer at the old Cheshire Cheese Restaurant in London. He once said to its manager, "Wilkins, I've dined here for years, but this is my last dinner with you. I finally rebel at the fact that your waiters are serving entirely too much tongue!"

No matter how long you have known a family or how long their attitude has been a friendly one, always continue to let them do most of the talking. By engaging them in unwarranted conversation, you lay yourself wide open to the possible feeling on their part that you are getting too familiar.

WHY SHOULD HE TAKE IT?

To "josh," to "kid," to nickname a customer, or to make personal remarks may poison him or her with resentment. They may take it for a while, but they probably do not like it and they do not have to take it. Sooner or later, they will stop dealing with "Familiarity & Co." Families *cannot* be taken for granted, and they resent deeply the familiar attitude which takes them for granted.

RESERVATION

The funeral profession expects and requires proper reserve that will keep you from becoming entangled in embarrassing situations. Such reserve is always an indication of refinement and good judgment. Those qualities play an important part in winning friends and families.

 DISCUSSION QUESTIONS

1. How have you been offended by someone's being too familiar with you?

2. List the possible risks of such behavior in funeral service.

3. Do you think being formal at a funeral is good or bad?

4. Do you think General MacArthur overreacted?

VII

OUR NOBLE PROFESSION
Inspirational Readings About Funeral Service

"The greatest use of life is to spend it on something that outlasts it."

William James

46

THE FUNERAL OF THE
UNKNOWN SOLDIER

"Only a life lived for others is a life worthwhile."
Albert Einstein

LEARNING OBJECTIVES

- Be able to describe the funeral of the Unknown Soldier.

- Define the idea of "people feeling they have done the right thing."

- Define the idea of "peace of mind."

- Understand why the basic purpose of the funeral is ultimately unexplainable.

Nowhere in the annals of history is the true, unblemished value of the funeral seen more than in the events surrounding the funeral of the Unknown Soldier.

At 8:30 A.M. on Armistice Day, November 11, 1921, gun salvos sounded from Fort Myer and continued every 60 seconds during the five-hour ceremony. No military leader who died in the course of any war, regardless of rank or achievements, received such a funeral as the soldier who on this day would be interred as the Unknown Soldier in America's most hallowed and revered cemetery, Arlington.

The ceremony was really symbolic of the eternal gratitude of the whole nation to the common soldiers who sacrificed their lives for our freedom.

NEVER FORGET.
SO MUCH HAS BEEN GIVEN...

While the nation honored this nameless man on that chilly November morning, the Unknown Soldier, whose body came on the caisson down Pennsylvania Avenue in front of thousands of mourners, was known to all. He was one of "our boys," an American son, not a warrior as they were called throughout the centuries in the dark days of war.

To some women that day, weeping in the crowd after an

all-night vigil, the Unknown Soldier was their boy who was missing one day and was never found, until now.

To many of the men who lined the route of the procession, wearing ribbons and badges of mourning on now civilian clothes, he was a familiar figure—a comrade, the one they liked best, maybe the one who went to their taverns, the one who went out into the fields of death and stayed there with the great, noble, and honored companionship.

As the funeral procession went by that day, a chilling thought entered the minds of many men: "That could have been me." Every man and woman that day undoubtedly realized that the funeral procession was a symbol of attained and cherished freedom and peace—that the world would now be a better place.

It was the red, white, and blue of Old Glory, draped over the gray military casket, that revealed him instantly, not as a mythical warrior aloof from common humanity, but as one of those fellows dressed in the drab of khaki, stained by mud and grease, who went into the ditches and dirty trenches with the flag leading his way. In his heart were unspoken emotions, bravery, and fear, with a faith not shaken. He was full of complication, but in the watchwords of that war, he and we were then under the same flag as we are now.

As the funeral procession reached the Arlington Cemetery amphitheater, there were some of the great men of the time waiting to greet the body of a simple soldier. General John J. "Black Jack" Pershing, tall and dignified, stood at attention, along with former presidents William Howard Taft and Woodrow Wilson, frail since being stricken by a stroke, but still the acknowledged and revered war leader. President Warren G. Harding nervously shuffled the papers of his speech.

There were presidents, bishops, archbishops, priests, and prime ministers ready to honor the body of a soldier who had gone trudging through the mud and muck like one ant in a legion of ants, unknown to fame. A casualty not more heroic than his pals around him, perhaps not missed much when he fell dead between the tangled wire and shell holes, but a hero nonetheless.

The body was brought before the greats of the greats from the U.S. military. It was their brains that had directed his movements down that long road that blistered his feet, over ground made impossible to cover because of gunfire, and up banks from which he slipped under the weight of his pack. Whatever his rank as a solider, this day marked the end of his journey, which this day finished in a grave marked "Unknown."

In life, the soldier had looked upon these great men in awe. Sometimes, he had saluted them as they rode past in their magnificence. Now, they all stood at Arlington to salute him, to keep their silence in his presence, to render him homage more wonderful, with deeper reverence than any general or president has ever received. It was noticed that of all the greats who on this funeral day were humbled, only Woodrow Wilson unashamedly shed tears.

The light was dim that morning at Arlington. The ruins of Arlington House, the former home of Robert E. Lee, now the center of the cemetery, looked gloomy in the November mist. The Capitol dome could not be seen but the minute guns along the funeral route kept booming. Soon, the sun shone brighter so that the dome of the Capitol was etched with ever-deepening lines. On all the buildings, flags were flying at half-mast. The military officers, who walked about with drawn swords, wore mourning crepe on their left arms.

Presently, they passed the word along, "Reverse arms," and in all the lines of the funeral procession, soldiers turned over rifles and bent their heads in homage.

It was very silent in Arlington. Before the ordered silence, the dense lines of people had kept their places without movement and spoke little in their long line of waiting. Then, as they caught their first glimpse of the caisson, they were solemnly quiet, all heads bared and bent. One could feel the spirit of the crowd. This gathering of everyday people was touched with a sharp, yet comforting thought as to what this funeral was all about: Freedom.

The military bands passed with their inspiring music and their drums thumping at the hearts of men, women, and children. Guards with their reversed arms passed, and then the caisson, with its team of horses, halted in front of the cemetery amphitheater where President Harding stood, and every hand was raised to salute the soldier who died so we might live, chosen by fate for this honor, which is in remembrance of the great Army patriots who went out with "our boy" to fight for his country.

President Harding laid his wreath on the casket and then stepped back again. Crowded behind the caisson in one long line was an immense column of men from all branches of the military, moving up slowly before coming to a halt. They were followed by other men in civilian clothes. Everywhere among them could be seen the most ancient of funeral tributes—flowers in the form of wreaths and crosses.

Then, all was still and the picture was complete, framing

in the wreath lying upon the flag-draped casket. The soul of the nation at its best, purified at this moment by emotion, was there in silence about the body of the man dubbed for eternity as the Unknown Soldier.

Funeral guns were being fired in the distance. They were not loud, more like the distant crackling of guns on a misty day in France, a day when there was "nothing to report," though a day, perhaps, this man had died.

It was a time of silence. What thoughts were in the minds of all the people only God knows, as they stood there for those minutes that seem more like hours.

In the midst of this silence, the crowd focused in reverent awe and attention on not only the Unknown Soldier but on one of the last true casualties of the Great War—Woodrow Wilson.

For as sure as the barbed wire tore one's hand in battle and the bullets would rip and tear at your very soul, so it was likened to this great man who had a mission of peace for all times, but for whose cause the barbed wire and bullets tore to pieces. Yes, there were two casualties of war on this Armistice Day.

Suddenly, the silence ended. Some words rang out and bugles could be heard sounding the three flourishes over the tomb, the ancient signal in war that the battle is over for the warrior but must continue for the rest who are alive.

In the crowd, women were weeping quietly, but it was their hearts crying that made the loudest sound. Men's faces were hard, like masks, hiding all they thought and felt.

At the entrance to the ceremonial platform, the casket was carried shoulder-high by eight tall military men. On the platform, the casket was centered in the pathway usually held for kings, prime ministers, and presidents. Now, no one can ever go to the altar of death to commemorate or to be honored without first paying homage to the resting place of the man who is a symbol of the many soldiers who died so that this nation might endure.

The actual service was as simple as in any village church in the land. The 23rd Psalm was sung, followed by an invocation and an address by President Harding. Then, another anthem and almost, as an afterthought, the program called for some brief remarks by President Woodrow Wilson.

The crowds hushed as the now invalid war leader was helped to the podium. President Wilson, with his head bowed and his wife bracing his paralyzed left side, said: "Our life is but a little span. One generation follows another very quickly. If a man with red blood in him had his choice, knowing that he must die, he would rather die to vindicate some right, unselfish to himself, than die in his own bed.

"This is what has brought us together today, for we all are touched with the love of the glory which is real glory, and the only real glory comes from utter self-forgetfulness and self-sacrifice. As impressive as this monument is, the true glory of the American experience is that we can never erect enough statues to men who have not been forgotten themselves and been glorified by the memory of others. This is the patriotic standard that America holds up to mankind in all sincerity and in all earnestness."

The crowd stood with moistened eyes in absolute silence. As the great man was helped from the platform, a cheer went up that lasted 10 minutes. It was to be the only applause of the day.

The gray metal casket was lowered into the tomb. A clergyman said something about "earth to earth" as President Taft stepped forward and, from a silver bowl, sprinkled the casket with soil from France. The service was concluded. The funeral ritual had accomplished its mystical and unexplainable purpose: It made people feel that they had done the right thing and gave them peace of mind.

As the words of blessing died away, from far up the line a whisper of sound could be heard. The sound grew louder and it seemed that all were on the march back to the joys and sorrows of daily life.

As the last person left, and the last roll of drums faded, two soldiers came forward to serve as the host guard for this glorious dead. From that day onward, there would forever be a guard at the tomb of "our boy," at the entrance to the hallowed tomb of the Unknown Soldier.

DISCUSSION QUESTIONS

1. What does the tomb of the Unknown Soldier mean to you?

2. What does "reverence for the dead" mean?

3. What happens when the dead are not cared for?

4. How did you feel after reading this chapter?

47

THE HONORABLE PROFESSION

"Honor is like the eye, which cannot suffer the least impurity without damage. It is a precious stone, the price of which is lessened by a single flaw."

Jacques Bénigne Bossuet

 LEARNING OBJECTIVES

- Understand the roles of the funeral director.
- Develop the idea of "indispensable service."
- Define the term *caretaker of the dead*.
- Define the term *caregiver to the living*.

Funeral directors perform an absolutely indispensable service for the living when death occurs. We are indeed professionals of the first rank.

As funeral directors, we wear many hats: advisor, helper, administrator, community leader, and friend, to name a few. We are caretakers of the dead and caregivers to the living. Few vocations carry such heavy responsibility.

We have all endured the fears, jokes, and comments of our friends and neighbors concerning our profession. To some extent, it is understandable: Death anxiety is an overwhelming emotion for most people. However, ours is an honorable profession, one deserving respect and understanding.

In this chapter, we will review the role of the funeral director.

WEAR THEM ALL, EVERY DAY.

THE ROLES OF THE FUNERAL DIRECTOR

Funeral directors perform five major roles: caretakers of the dead, caregivers to the living, compassionate advisor, administrator, and community leader.

Caretakers of the Dead

When people die, they are unable to personally defend their own dignity and honor. As caretakers of the dead, funeral professionals are guided by the solemn pledge that all deceased persons, regardless of the cause of death, will be prepared for the chosen form of disposition in the most ethical manner, professionally and technically. The deceased's appearance will last in the minds of the survivors for many years. As funeral directors, we pledge to give the bereaved a guarantee that the best possible results will be sought through the finest embalming and treatment techniques available.

Remember: Our professional role becomes sacred when a bereaved family entrusts us with their precious, beloved family member. We must continually earn the faith and trust of the family by treating the body reverently.

Caregivers to the Living

The second major role of funeral directors is to serve as caregivers to the living. We pledge time, talent, and energies in fulfilling the expressed desires of the bereaved family. We are committed to encouraging the healthy expression of grief through the use of time-honored funeral rituals and accompanying religious ceremonies. In doing so, we respect, honor, and cooperate with attending clergy. Their guidance is indispensable to finding value in the funeral ritual and, therefore, must not be hindered or slowed for the convenience of the funeral home or director.

Compassionate Advisor

Grief is perhaps the most overwhelming emotion experienced by a human being. When a significant person dies, the funeral director must calmly minister to the emotions, confusion, and chaos even in the most tragic and distasteful circumstances. This care and compassion can know no prejudice. The emotional needs of the poor are as great as those of the rich of any class, religion, sex, or nationality.

Administrator

Funeral directors are organizational specialists. This applies to both administering the funeral home and ministering to the needs of the families. Funeral directors believe in the concept of the funeral as an organized, purposeful, time-limited, flexible, group-centered response to death and as such must be handled with efficiency, compassion, propriety, and dignity.

We are highly motivated to comply fully with all local, state, federal, and provincial regulations pertaining to funeral service in particular and the community in general.

At the same time, practitioners of funeral services see the funeral ritual as a crucial aspect in adjustment made by the bereaved and the community. When grief engulfs a family, the funeral director must provide every means of support possible to ensure that all necessary paperwork is completed, services are selected, and disposition is arranged.

Community Leader

Funeral directors are dedicated to the communities they serve. The fellowship they establish with their neighbors and friends is beneficial to the community and the funeral home. Community participation reflects the funeral director's professionalism and humanity.

Funeral directors are honorable professionals dedicated to the dignity of humankind in both life and death. Final rites, tributes, and the hallowed dignity of the funeral service serve to honor life. Memorialization of the dead acknowledges the fact that a life has been lived and has now ended. Opportunities to remember and honor the dead are implemented throughout our profession. We must therefore always respect our time-honored traditions while giving enlightened and competent guidance and support to the bereaved.

 DISCUSSION QUESTIONS

1. Discuss whether funeral service is a trade or a profession. Write down your conclusion.

2. How do you define *caretaker of the dead*?

3. Analyze this idea: Funerals are for the living.

4. Discuss what honor means.

48

CODE OF PROFESSIONAL ETHICS FOR THE FUNERAL SERVICE PRACTITIONER

"If it is not right, do not do it; if it is not true do not say it."

Marcus Aurelius

LEARNING OBJECTIVES

- Understand what a code of ethics represents.
- Be able to explain what the term *custodian of the funeral* means.
- Understand the ethical significance of the clergy–funeral director relationship.
- Be able to explain the ethical significance of the concept of "disclosure."

I believe in the concept of the funeral as an organized, purposeful, time-limited, flexible, group-centered response to death. I believe the funeral to be a crucial aspect in the adjustment made by the bereaved, and the community at large, when the death of a significant other occurs. My decision to become a licensed funeral service practitioner voiced acceptance of the responsibility to be a custodian of the funeral rituals that are implemented to commemorate the fact that a life has been lived.

The dead will be cared for and disposed of with the highest level of dignity and respect possible. To allow for the final mourning period, I pledge to prepare any deceased person, regardless of cause of death (with proper authorizations), in the best manner professionally and technically possible. As the deceased's appearance will last for many years in the memories of the survivors, they deserve nothing less than the guarantee that I will labor for their behalf in furnishing the best possible results through the use of the finest embalming techniques available.

I pledge to function as a caregiver to my clientele. I will dedicate my time, talents, and energy toward fulfilling their expressed desires regarding the funeral and the care of their decedent. I will also adapt my ideas and funeral facilities to their needs and desires, in order to meet the end result of being a help (and not a hindrance) in their mourning process. I will strive with any means at my disposal to assist the healthy expression of grief, and the beginning resolution of grief through the use of rites, rituals, and ceremonies.

Never will any property or personal effects of the decedent be mishandled. The discretion of the family or survivors will be explicitly followed in the return or the authorized disposition of material effects. No intentional desecration of personal property will ever occur.

The clergy for the funeral will be honored and cooperated with implicitly. Religious expression, under the clergy and family guidance, will never be hindered for the convenience of the funeral establishment or myself.

All business conducted under my professional guidance shall be in full compliance with all federal, state, and local laws and regulations. Full disclosure of any and all pricing schedules will be granted upon request.

No pricing or professional practice will involve misrepresentations of undisclosed costs. All honoraria, funeral goods, service charges, and items for which we act in full or part in agency for the client will be itemized and explained fully. We will allow all optional offerings to be selected or rejected, per the client's wishes.

I pledge that I will service not only my clients but also my community. If I aid in increasing knowledge concerning death, the value of the funeral and its societal role, or the healthy satisfaction of the grieving process, then I have at that time fulfilled my purpose as a funeral service practitioner.

DISCUSSION QUESTIONS

1. Make a list of all the ethical goods you can think of concerning funeral service.

2. Discuss the ethical impact funeral service has on a community.

3. How many codes of ethics have you ever pledged to? Do you think this is important or not?

4. Write your own code of ethics.

49

A WINNING PERSONALITY

Alfred Bickford Marsh
Funeral Director 1906–1974

"Throw away the rod, throw away the wrath; take the
gentle path."
George Herbert

 LEARNING OBJECTIVES

- Be able to identify role models in funeral service.
- Understand the qualities that generate goodwill.
- Understand the meaning of professional immortality.
- Appreciate your own impact on the attitudes of others.

QUALITIES THAT WIN GOODWILL

One of the greatest blessings that I have had in my career as a funeral director is the fact that I learned this profession early on from a few men that today I call Great American Funeral Directors. This is the story of one of these veteran funeral directors. His name was Alfred Bickford Marsh, and I worked for him my first year in mortuary college.

Everyone called him "Al," and he used to say he was "part American and part just plain folks." Whatever his combination, it was a winning one. People just liked Al. He was a mighty fine person! He had a heartwarming smile, a dry wit, and a way of inspiring enthusiasm that I try to retain to this very day.

Al Marsh loved being a funeral director. He said he liked the term undertaker better because he thought it defined what the profession was all about more accurately—the person who undertook the task of caring for the dead and the living. He would always smile and ask, "Well, why aren't we called undertooker's then?"

What made Mr. Marsh special was his winning personality. Every grave digger, every florist, and every vault man considered Al a personal friend.

Let's look at the different elements of Mr. Marsh's personality to discover how we can adopt them ourselves.

HE WAS SINCERE

Even his joking was sincere, for he "kidded" to change some condition or opinion which, to him, was wrong or ill advised. He had a natural sweetness of character that enabled him to say and do things without offending others. It was not the artificial sweet flavor of fake sugar, which merely tastes sweet and has no substance, but more like good, old-fashioned maple sugar. There was nourishment for all who knew him in the wholesome sweetness of his character.

HIS LIKING FOR PEOPLE WAS NO MERE AFFECTATION

Everywhere Al went he kept a pocket full of quarters. As he walked around town, he would always hand quarters to children, and many, many times the quarters would turn into $10 and $20 bills when he encountered some street person or a person really down on his luck.

There would always be a brief word. Al would take out some money, and the figure would move away. I remember one man asked Al why he gave so much cash away, and Mr. Marsh replied that he was just paying off some debts that *he* owed. I always thought these disbursements ran into hundreds of dollars a week.

ALWAYS LOYAL TO HIS AGREEMENTS

One night a funeral home in Albany called us to do a trade embalming. The Albany funeral director gave us just the details about the death and little else as information was concerned.

The trip from Albany to our town was about two hours, so by the time we had made the removal and had finished the embalming, the Albany director was at our doorstep.

"How are you this morning?" Mr. Marsh asked. "Not so great," was the reply. "You know this woman hasn't got a dime and the funeral is going to be on the county; there is no money to do much of anything."

I could see the look on Mr. Marsh's face. He knew that the funeral director from Albany probably knew the situation when he called. He also knew that to keep the cost down, this funeral director should have not engaged us but done the work himself. As it was, we got out of bed at 5:00 A.M. while this gentleman got four more hours of sleep.

Then, a big smile came over Mr. Marsh. "Well, not to worry! You know, my young man here (meaning me) knows little if anything about embalming. This was a great learning experience for him, and you know there is no charge for this trade work because I would rather have your friendship than your money!"

The funeral director from Albany was clearly taken aback by Mr. Marsh's response and generosity and I think a little embarrassed. I just stood there looking at Mr. Marsh and thought, "Hot damn, that's how I want to be when I grow up!"

GENUINE—ENTIRELY!

Mr. Marsh never put on airs. He usually wore a plain blue suit and drove an old Plymouth Fury II, but when he dressed for a funeral he would "back up into the harness." The harness was his funeral suit, and he was a sight to behold. He wore a starched white shirt, black onyx cuff links, grey and white striped tie, black vest and coat, grey and black striped pants, polished black shoes, and black socks. He wore a Prince Albert coat and homburg hat in the winter, and for summer funerals he got a little less formal and did not wear his vest.

He had a marvelous singing voice and was a member of the prestigious Handel–Haydn Society of the Boston Symphony Orchestra, and on funerals Al had a unique way of leaving an impression on people.

As the organist was playing, Al would extend his arm to usher a lady to her seat, and while they were walking together Al would begin to sing the lyrics of the song the organist was playing. He literally would serenade the ladies.

The first time I saw him do this, I thought Al was the most

eccentric and odd funeral director I had ever seen. If the ushering got backed up and I went over and extended my arm to a lady, invariably her response would be, "I'll wait for Mr. Marsh."

I learned three lessons from that experience: (1) people like to be sung to, (2) they really liked Mr. Marsh, and (3) I wanted to be like Mr. Marsh!

PROFESSIONAL IMMORTALITY

Alfred Bickford Marsh, a Great American Funeral Director, has been dead many years, but his influence and style are immortalized professionally by those of us who were honored and privileged to have him as our mentor. One of the most fortunate things that I have had happen in my life was to have him as my mentor.

I hear people complain that they can't get along because they have no "pull." I learned from Al Marsh that the greatest pull anyone can have is within oneself—the development of a pleasing and winning personality. Without that, Alfred B. Marsh would have been just another funeral director in a long line of other funeral directors.

I believe we can all stand out in our own sphere and achieve professional immortality by emphasizing in our own personalities those same qualities that won Alfred B. Marsh such affection.

This is a truly great profession, and you, too, can demonstrate a sweetness of character. You can be thoughtful of others. You can be loyal to your agreements, and you, too, can be genuine without affectation. It is the swiftest and surest way to win the goodwill and cooperation of everyone with whom you deal.

Thanks, Al. Your memory lives on.

 DISCUSSION QUESTIONS

1. Have you ever encountered a Great American Funeral Director? If so, describe his or her personality.

2. Talk about being sincere in your liking of people. How important is this?

3. What are the benefits of being genuine and loyal?

4. How do you want people to talk about you after you are dead?

50

"THE UNDERTAKER"

"Poets are all who love and feel great truths, and tell them."

Gamaliel Bailey

LEARNING OBJECTIVES

- Define the term *matter of the heart.*

- Understand the poetry of funeral service.

- Appreciate the gentleness and sensitivity that funeral service requires.

- Understand the inherent greatness of the funeral service profession.

This poem, written many years ago, expresses eloquently the reality and focus of this great profession. There is a gentleness and a dignity about funeral service, and no one better describes gentle and dignified aspects of life than the poet. The poet who wrote these lines attempted to speak to matters of the heart—and if funeral service is anything, it is a *matter of the heart.*

    This poem was originally given to me by Norbert L. Blust, who was a long-time funeral director in my hometown in Iowa.

"The Undertaker"

The midnight hour, the darkest hour
That human grief may know,
Sends forth its hurried summons—
Ask me to come—I go!

I know not when the bell may toll,
I know not where the blow may fall,
I only know that I must go
In answer to the call.

Perhaps a friend—perhaps unknown—
'Tis fate that turns the wheel—
The tangled skein of human life
Winds slowly on the reel.

And I?—I'm the undertaker,
"Cold-Blooded," you'll hear them say,
"Trained to the shock and chill of death,
With a heart that's cold and grey."

Trained—that's what they call it
How little they know the rest—
I'm human, and know the sorrow
That throbs in the aching breast.

Bennett Chapple

DISCUSSION QUESTIONS

1. How have you experienced grief?

2. Discuss the mission of funeral service.

3. Why do people often criticize and ridicule funeral directors?

4. What do you have to offer this great profession?

INDEX

ABOUT THE AUTHOR

Todd W. Van Beck is a noted author, lecturer and seminar leader in the areas of funeral service, cemetery work, and clergy activities. He is a graduate of The New England Institute at Mount Ida College, the Mount Mercy College, Mount Saint Mary's Seminary and has attended Boston University. Mr. Van Beck is also a Certified Funeral Service Practitioner with the Academy of Professional Funeral Service Practice and is Dean of the Funeral College at the University of Memphis for the International Cemetery and Funeral Association. He is also an active member of The National Funeral Director's Association. Mr. Van Beck has one son and lives in Cincinnati, Ohio.

Printed in the United States
26608LVS00005B/55-255